STEPS TO A FEARLESS BIRTH

By

Samsarah Morgan CD LC Cht

With a foreword by Ibu Robin Lim

Urban Nana Publishing, Oakland, CA
Copyright 2023

Table of Contents

Diabetes prevents the body from digesting and using the glucose it consumes. There are several types of diabetes, each with its own symptoms and causes, but they all have one thing in common: an elevated blood glucose level. Insulin and/or medications can be used to treat this condition. It is possible to prevent certain types of diabetes by adopting a healthy lifestyle.

Diabetes Mellitus, also referred to as Type 1 diabetes, is a metabolic disorder characterized by abnormally high blood glucose levels. The onset of diabetes occurs when sugar is transported from the bloodstream into the cells, where it can be stored or utilized for energy production. Insulin is a hormone that the pancreas produces. Diabetes is a condition in which the body either does not produce enough insulin or cannot effectively utilize the insulin it does produce.

If you do not control your diabetes-related high blood sugar, your nerves, kidneys, eyes, and other organs may be damaged.

The onset of diabetes symptoms is triggered by an increase in blood sugar levels.

In addition, diabetes manifests as increased appetite and thirst, weight loss, frequent urination, impaired vision, extreme fatigue, and non-healing wounds.

Multiple factors, including your environment, family, and preexisting medical conditions, can influence your diabetes risk.

Patients with diabetes must therefore be mindful of what they eat and how much they consume.

Several factors, including weight gain, can exacerbate the disease, making it even more crucial for diabetic patients to maintain a healthy lifestyle and control their weight.

A higher incidence of Type 1 diabetes, also known as adult-onset diabetes or insulin resistance, is associated with obesity. In this condition, the glucose level in the blood is consistently elevated. In obese individuals, fat tissue cells may metabolize more calories than they can consume. Inflammation stimulates a protein called cytokinesis, which is triggered by stress in these cells, when excessive nutrients are consumed. Consequently, cytokines inhibit insulin receptor signaling, causing cells to develop insulin resistance over time. Insulin encourages cells to utilize glucose for sustenance. Due to the fact that your cells are insulin-resistant, your body will be unable to convert glucose into energy, resulting in a persistently high blood glucose level. In addition to reducing normal insulin responses, stress frequently causes inflammation of cells and may contribute to heart failure. Obesity or overweight increases the risk of Type 1 diabetes, which occurs when the body's cells develop insulin resistance despite sufficient insulin levels. The insides of human cells are burdened by excess weight. When there are more nutrients to absorb than the cells can manage, the cell membrane sends a warning signal instructing the cells to reduce the number of insulin cell surface receptors.

Insulin resistance and persistently elevated blood glucose levels are two of the most evident diabetes symptoms. Patients with diabetes are more likely than non-diabetic patients to develop severe heart conditions like diabetic cardiomyopathy, coronary artery disease, and heart failure. Due to the accumulation of fatty substances in the arteries, the heart of obese or diabetic individuals must work harder to pump blood throughout the body.

Obese individuals, and Type 1 diabetics in particular, must lose weight in order to improve their health. A moderate and consistent weight loss of at least 5-10% will increase insulin activity, decrease fasting blood glucose levels, and reduce the need for certain diabetes medications. In addition, you must monitor your lifestyle in order to alleviate diabetes symptoms or, at the very least, to reduce your risk of developing diabetes.

Nutritional balance and health Physical exercise Medications Just as important as medication is physical activity, but an air fryer can help you maintain a healthy and balanced diet. You can lose weight by regulating your diet and analyzing the effects of your eating on your body.

This book contains everything you need to know about diabetes, including what to eat and avoid in this condition.

You will also find a number of simple, low-carbohydrate recipes that help you maintain your blood sugar level and insulin levels to combat diabetes.

I t is a chronic condition that develops when the pancreas cannot produce enough insulin to meet the body's needs, or when the insulin it does produce is not utilized properly by the body. Insulin is the hormone responsible for regulating blood sugar levels.

Types of Diabetes

There are different types of diabetes:

Type 1 Diabetes

Insulin-dependent diabetes or juvenile diabetes is caused by a deficiency in the immune system or an autoimmune disease. Your immune system attacks insulin-producing pancreatic cells, preventing the body from producing insulin. It is unknown what causes autoimmune disease and how to effectively treat it. To live with Type 1 diabetes, however, insulin must be taken.

Type 2 Diabetes

Adult-onset diabetes, also known as non-insulin-dependent diabetes, is caused by inadequate insulin utilization by the body. The vast majority of diabetics suffer from Type 1 diabetes. The symptoms are frequently misdiagnosed as Type 1 diabetes. However, the issue can be identified after several years of diagnosis, which is significantly less obvious when symptoms have already manifested. When your blood sugar levels rise and your body becomes resistant to insulin, Type 1 diabetes develops. Insulin

resistance is the cause of Type 1 diabetes. This is the cause of obesity. In addition, the pancreas fails to utilize insulin properly in Type 1 diabetes. This complicates the process of removing sugar from the blood and storing it as energy in the cells. Consequently, the demand for insulin therapy will increase.

Gestational Diabetes

Gestational diabetes is defined as hyperglycemia, or blood glucose levels that are elevated but not high enough to qualify as diabetes. Gestational diabetes is diagnosed using prenatal tests rather than symptoms such as high blood sugar that can develop during pregnancy. Placental hormones that inhibit insulin are the primary cause of this form of diabetes. This type of diabetes is caused by substances produced by the placenta that inhibit insulin.

Causes of Diabetes

Causes of Type 1 Diabetes

Type 1 diabetes has no known cause. One hypothesis is that pancreatic insulin-producing cells are targeted and eliminated by the immune system. In general, the immune system destroys viruses and infectious bacteria. In the human body, insulin levels are negligible or nonexistent. Consequently, sugar accumulates in the blood rather than being transported to the cells. Although the exact nature of these factors is unknown, it is believed that Type 1 diabetes is caused by a combination of genetic predisposition and environmental influences. In Type 1 diabetes, weight is considered irrelevant. Type 1 diabetes develops when the immune system (the body's ability to fight disease) targets and destroys the insulin-producing beta cells in the pancreas. According to scientists, Type 1 diabetes is influenced by both genetic and environmental factors.

Causes of Prediabetes and Type 2 Diabetes

In prediabetes, as in Type 1 diabetes, your cells can become resistant to the effects of insulin, and the pancreas cannot produce enough insulin to overcome this resistance. Therefore, sugar accumulates

in the bloodstream as opposed to being transported to the cells, where it would be required as fuel. Although genetic and environmental factors are believed to play a role in the development of Type 1 diabetes, the underlying cause is unknown. Obesity is associated with the progression of Type 1 diabetes, although not all patients are obese. The most prevalent form of diabetes is caused by several factors:

1. **Genes and family history**

   Diabetes in the family increases the likelihood that a mother will develop gestational diabetes, suggesting that genes play a role. Mutations may also explain why the disease is more prevalent in Asians, African Americans, American Indians, and Hispanic women. Any gene may increase the likelihood of developing Type 1 or Type 1 diabetes. In addition, a person's genetic background can contribute to obesity and Type 1 diabetes.

2. **Overweight, physical inactivity, and obesity**

   You are significantly more likely to develop Type 1 diabetes if you do not regularly engage in physical activity and if you are obese or overweight. Insulin resistance, which is prevalent in people with Type 1 diabetes, is frequently caused by obesity. In which the fat deposits of the body play a significant role. Insulin resistance, Type 1 diabetes, heart disease, and blood vessel disease are all associated with excess abdominal fat.

3. **Insulin resistance**

   Insulin resistance, a condition in which the body, liver, and fat cells do not effectively process insulin, is a common complication of Type 1 diabetes. Consequently, the body requires more insulin to transport glucose to cells. In order to meet the increased demand, the pancreas produces more insulin. However, over time, the pancreas loses its ability to produce insulin, resulting in an increase in blood glucose levels.

Difference between Type 1 and Type 1 Diabetes

Type 1 diabetes is an autoimmune disease. In this condition, the immune system destroys the cells that produce insulin, preventing the body from producing any insulin. Type 1 diabetes typically manifests in childhood and can last a lifetime.

Weight and lethargy are lifestyle and genetic factors that cause Type 1 diabetes. Frequently, diet and exercise can reverse or ameliorate the condition, which typically manifests in adulthood. 90-95 percent of people diagnosed with diabetes have Type 1 diabetes.

How to Prevent Diabetes

Modifications to one's lifestyle can prevent Type 1 diabetes, the most common form of the disease. If you have an increased risk for Type 1 diabetes due to excessive weight gain and obesity, high blood cholesterol, or a positive family history, prevention is essential.

If you have prediabetes, which is high blood sugar but not high enough to be classified as diabetes, modifying your lifestyle can help you prevent or delay the onset of the disease.

A few changes to your lifestyle now may help you avoid diabetes-related complications in the future, such as nerve, kidney, and heart damage. Never is it too late to begin something new.

Get rid of any excess weight.

If you lose weight, your risk of developing diabetes decreases. In one extensive study, for instance, people reduced their risk of developing diabetes by nearly 60% after losing approximately 7% of their body weight through exercise and dietary changes.

Establish a weight loss objective proportional to your current weight. Discuss with your physician setting reasonable short-term objectives, such as losing one to two pounds per week.

Increase your physical activity.

The benefits of regular physical activity are numerous. Physical activity can benefit you in the following ways:

Reduce your weight, lower your blood sugar, and increase your insulin sensitivity to help maintain a healthy blood sugar level.

Consume a variety of plant-based foods.

Plants are a source of vitamins, minerals, and carbohydrates. Carbohydrates contain sugars and starches that supply the body with energy and fiber. However, dietary fiber is the portion of plant foods that cannot be absorbed or digested by the body.

Dietary fiber helps you lose weight and reduces your risk of developing diabetes. Consume a variety of wholesome, fiber-rich meals.

Among its many benefits, fiber slows sugar absorption and lowers blood sugar levels.

Consume a variety of healthful fats.

Fat-rich foods are high in calories and should be consumed in moderation. For weight loss and management, your diet should include a variety of foods rich in unsaturated fats, also known as "healthy fats."

Both polyunsaturated and monounsaturated fats promote healthy cholesterol levels in the blood.

Dairy and animal products are sources of saturated fats, also known as "bad fats." However, you should limit these foods to a small portion of your diet. Low-fat dairy products, lean poultry, and lean pork are excellent sources of saturated fats.

Avoid trendy diets in favor of healthier alternatives.

Many fad diets, including the glycemic index, paleo, and keto diets, can help you lose weight. However, there is limited evidence of the long-term benefits of these diets or their ability to prevent diabetes.

How to Control Sugar Level

Finding an acceptable compromise between the drugs you take (insulin or tablets), what you eat, and the amount of exercise you get is the key to managing diabetes. A problem with anyone could cause an increase or decrease in blood sugar levels. Several factors typically contribute to abnormal blood glucose levels. We list some of them below, but do not claim to cover all of them:

- Failure to adhere to the dietary guidelines (e.g., eating too much or too little food without taking into account the recommendations)
- Failure to engage in regular physical activity
- Excessive stress
- Inability to control blood glucose levels

Regularly track your blood sugar levels and note when they are too high or too low. Thus, your diabetic team can more efficiently make any necessary adjustments to your diabetes treatment plan.

It is not always simple to maintain blood sugar levels near normal, and no one has perfect blood sugar control. Even if you do everything possible to stabilize your blood sugar levels, they may fluctuate occasionally.

However, there are a few things you can do to maintain healthy blood sugar levels:

- When taking insulin or tablets, adhere to the prescribed schedule.
- Stick as closely as possible to your diet plan.
- Maintain a regular exercise regimen.

- Check your blood sugar levels multiple times per day.
- You should visit your physician frequently.
- Learn as much as possible about diabetes.

If you adhere to these guidelines, you will do everything possible to keep your disease under control.

Here Is How Your Blood Glucose Level Should Look Like

Mg/DL	Fasting	After Eating	2-3 hours After Eating
Normal	80-100	170-200	120-140
Impaired Glucose	101-125	190-230	140-160
Diabetic	126 +	220-300	200 +

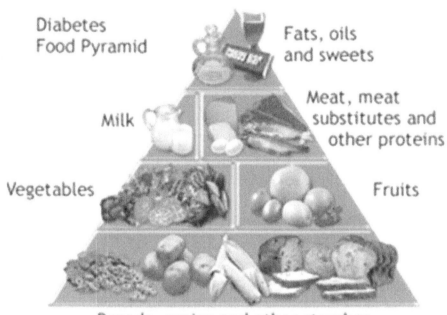

Diabetes Food Pyramid

Fats, oils and sweets

Milk

Meat, meat substitutes and other proteins

Vegetables

Fruits

Breads, grains and other starches

Nutritional Goals for Type 1 Diabetes

Manage your weight

To give yourself a good chance of successfully managing Type 2 diabetes while preventing some of the many health risks it presents, you must maintain a healthy body mass index. By losing weight, obese individuals can better manage their diabetes, lower their blood pressure, and reduce blood fat levels, including cholesterol. Diet and exercise are the two most important factors in weight control. This book will help you adopt a healthier diet and track your caloric intake so you can determine how much energy you should be expending through exercise.

Balance the blood glucose level

Maintaining healthy blood glucose levels is essential for managing diabetes. Over time, an excessive amount of glucose in the blood can damage the blood vessels that supply the heart, kidneys, eyes, and nerves. Blood glucose levels are determined primarily by the type and quantity of carbohydrates consumed. Slow-release carbohydrates maintain steady blood glucose levels, whereas rapidly digested carbohydrates cause undesirable spikes in blood glucose levels.

Take care of your heart

Individuals with diabetes are five times more likely to develop complications from heart disease or a stroke, so it is essential to consume the proper foods to maintain a healthy heart. Reducing your consumption of saturated fat is one of the most crucial steps you can take. Saturated fat induces cholesterol production in the body. In the same way that hard water can clog pipes and appliances with limescale, cholesterol clogs and narrows blood vessels, restricting blood flow to the heart and brain.

Control Blood pressure

Increases the risk of cardiovascular disease, stroke, and kidney disease. A diet high in sodium contributes significantly to the development of hypertension, but sodium is not the only factor. The DASH (Dietary Approaches to Stop Hypertension) study conducted in the United States discovered that people who had a moderate sodium intake but increased their intake of potassium, calcium, and magnesium by eating an abundance of fruits, vegetables, and low-fat dairy products had greater reductions in blood pressure than those who restricted sodium intake. So ask your doctor to regularly monitor your blood pressure.

Eat more fruits and vegetables

Vegetables and fruits are the pillars of a diabetes-friendly diet. They provide vitamins, minerals, and phytochemicals that, among other benefits, promote heart and eye health; potassium, which lowers blood pressure; and dietary fiber, which promotes digestive health.

Choose the right carbohydrates

The conversion of carbohydrates to glucose raises the blood glucose concentration. The level it reaches and the length of time it remains elevated depend on the type and quantity of carbohydrates you consume. Certain carbohydrates break down more slowly than others, thereby maintaining stable blood glucose levels and sustaining energy. Understanding the impact of carbohydrates on blood glucose levels is essential for diabetes management.

Swap bad fats for good

Reduce your consumption of saturated and trans fats, which increase the risk of cardiovascular disease and stroke. Instead, consume more protective "good fats" such as unsaturated oils.

Replace salt with good flavorings

It is believed that a diet high in sodium contributes significantly to the development of high blood pressure, which poses an increased risk for people with diabetes. On the other hand, according to experts, reducing sodium intake to less than 2.4 grams per day can reduce the risk of stroke or heart attack by 25 percent. Instead of relying on salt to add flavor to food, use alternative methods.

Lower the sugar intake

Sugar contains what nutritionists refer to as "empty calories" — calories that provide no protein, fiber, vitamins, or minerals and have no health benefits. Eating a lot of sugar will cause your blood

glucose levels to rise and can result in weight gain over time. You do not have to completely avoid sugar, but you should reduce your intake as much as possible and experiment with alternative sweeteners.

How Much You should Eat

Your nutritional goal should be to lose weight and maintain that loss in the future. Consequently, healthy eating habits must involve a method you can adhere to for the rest of your life. Choosing nutritious foods that complement some of your cuisines and traditional preferences could be advantageous.

Using a divided plate is a simple way to help you make healthy food choices and consume the proper portion sizes.

These three elements on your plate promote healthy eating:

- The majority of your plate should consist of fruits and non-starchy vegetables.
- Whole grains make up one-fourth of the diet.
- One-fourth of the diet consists of protein-rich foods, such as beans, seafood, and lean meats.

What to Eat?

Choose a diet rich in nutrient-dense foods if you have Type 1 diabetes in order to help your body get the vitamins, minerals, and fiber it needs.

Include in your diet monounsaturated and polyunsaturated fatty acids and other heart-healthy fats.

Similarly, consuming a variety of high-fiber foods may help control blood sugar levels and keep you feeling fuller for longer, preventing you from eating when you're not hungry.

Additionally, your diet should be simple to adhere to and maintain. Diets that are too restrictive or do not correspond with one's lifestyle can be difficult to maintain over time.

The following foods should be incorporated into your diet:

- Vegetables (broccoli, cauliflower, spinach, cucumbers, zucchini)
- Legumes (beans, lentils, chickpeas)
- Seeds (chia seeds, pumpkin seeds
- Fruits (apples, oranges, berries, melons, pears, peaches)
- Whole grains (quinoa, couscous, oats, brown rice, emmer)
- Nuts (almonds, walnuts, pistachios, macadamia nuts, cashews)
- Liquids (water, black coffee, unsweetened tea, vegetable juice).

What to Avoid Eating?

Beverages with added sugar

Sugary beverages are the worst beverages for diabetics to consume.

There are 38.5 g of carbohydrates in a 12-ounce (354 mL) can of cola.

Both sugary lemonade and iced tea contain approximately 45 grams of sugar-only carbohydrates.

In addition, these beverages contain a high amount of fructose, which is associated with diabetes and insulin resistance. According to research, the consumption of sugar-sweetened beverages increases the risk of diabetes-related conditions such as fatty liver disease.

In addition, the high fructose content of sweetened beverages may cause metabolic changes that promote abdominal fat and potentially dangerous triglyceride and cholesterol levels.

Instead of sugary beverages, drink club soda, water, or unsweetened iced tea to manage blood sugar levels and reduce the risk of disease.

Trans fats

Synthesized trans fatty acids are extremely hazardous.

Hydrogen is added to unsaturated fatty acids to make them more persistent.

Trans fats are present in margarine, peanut butter, spreads, frozen dinners, and creamers. In addition, they are commonly added to crackers, muffins, and other baked goods to extend their shelf life.

Despite not directly affecting blood sugar, trans fats have been linked to increased insulin resistance, inflammation, and abdominal fat, as well as lower levels of good cholesterol and impaired vascular function.

Avoid all products containing the phrase "partially hydrogenated" in the list of ingredients.

Pasta, white bread, and rice

High-carbohydrate processed foods include rice, white bread, and pasta.

The consumption of bagels, bread, and other refined-flour products has been shown to significantly increase blood sugar levels in individuals with Type 1 and Type 1 diabetes.

This reaction is not limited to products containing refined white flour. In one study, it was found that gluten-free pasta also raises blood sugar levels, with rice-based varieties having the greatest effect.

In a separate study, individuals with mental impairments and Type 1 diabetes who consumed a high-carbohydrate diet had elevated blood sugar levels and diminished brain function.

There is little fiber in these processed foods. Fiber slows the absorption of sugar into the bloodstream.

Increased fiber consumption augments the gut microbiota, which may reduce insulin resistance.

Yogurt with fruit flavors

People with diabetes could benefit from consuming plain yogurt. In contrast, fruit-flavored versions are a different story.

Typically made with nonfat or low-fat milk, flavored yogurts are high in sugar and carbohydrates.

Frozen yogurt is commonly considered a healthier alternative to ice cream. However, it can hold as much or more sugar than ice cream.

Instead of selecting high-sugar yogurts and risking insulin and blood sugar spikes, choose plain, whole-milk yogurt, which contains no added sugar and may aid in appetite control, weight loss, and gastrointestinal health.

Breakfast cereals with added sugar

Cereal is one of the most hazardous breakfast options for diabetics.

The majority of cereals are heavily processed and contain significantly more carbohydrates than most consumers realize, despite the health claims on their labels.

In addition, they contain a small amount of protein that can help you feel fuller throughout the day while maintaining stable blood sugar levels.

Even "healthy" breakfast cereals are discouraged for diabetics.

Avoid most cereals in favor of a low-carb, protein-based breakfast to regulate appetite and blood sugar.

Coffee drinks with different flavors

Coffee has been associated with numerous health benefits, including a lower incidence of diabetes.

In contrast, flavored coffee drinks should be considered a treat rather than a healthy beverage.

According to studies, the brain processes solid and liquid foods differently. As a result, when you consume calories, you do not compensate by eating less in the future, which can lead to weight gain.

Carbohydrates are abundant in flavored coffee beverages.

Choose espresso or regular coffee with a tablespoon of half-and-half or heavy cream to control your blood sugar and avoid weight gain.

Honey, maple syrup, and agave nectar

People with diabetes avoid white sugar and sweets such as cookies, candies, and pies.

However, other types of sugar can increase blood sugar levels. Examples include brown sugar and "natural" sugars such as honey, maple syrup, and agave nectar.

Although these sweeteners are not highly processed, they contain roughly the same amount of carbohydrates as white sugar. However, the majority have significantly more.

Avoiding all forms of sugar and replacing it with low-carb natural sweeteners is the most effective strategy.

Fruit that has been dried

Potassium, vitamin C, and other essential minerals and vitamins are abundant in fruit.

Fruit is dried, resulting in a lack of moisture and increased amounts of essential nutrients.

Unfortunately, the sugar content increases as well.

Raisins contain over four times as many carbohydrates as grapes. Carbohydrate Content of other dried fruit varieties is comparable to that of fresh fruit.

Diabetes does not necessitate complete abstinence from fruit. Adhering to low-sugar foods, such as a small apple or fresh berries, will assist you in maintaining a healthy blood sugar level within the target range.

Snacks in packages

Snacks like crackers, pretzels, and other types of prepared foods are not recommended.

They are typically made with refined flour and contain few nutrients, but are high in rapidly digestible carbohydrates that cause a rapid rise in blood sugar.

According to one study, snack foods contain an average of 7.7% more carbohydrates than their labels indicate.

If you are hungry between meals, almonds or low-carb vegetables with cheese are superior options.

Juice from fruits

Although fruit juice is commonly perceived as a healthy beverage, its effects on blood sugar are identical to those of other sugary beverages and sodas. This applies to both 100 percent unsweetened fruit juice and fruit juice with added sugar. Moreover, in some instances, fruit juice contains more carbohydrates and sugar than soda.

Like sugar-sweetened beverages, fruit juice is high in fructose. Fructose causes obesity, insulin resistance, and heart disease.

The best option is water with a slice of lemon, as it contains less than one gram of carbohydrates and is nearly calorie-free.

French Fries

French fries are one of the foods you should avoid if you have diabetes.

Potatoes have a relatively high carbohydrate content.

Fried potatoes may do more than raise blood sugar levels.

Multiple studies have linked frequent consumption of french fries and other fried foods to cancer and heart disease.

If you do not wish to eliminate potatoes, a small portion of sweet potatoes is the perfect substitute.

Breakfast

Vegetable Frittata

Preparation:
15 Minutes

Servings:
2

Directions:

1. Turn on the 375°F oven.
2. Whisk eggs in a medium bowl until they are well-beaten.
3. Olive oil is used to sauté onion, bell pepper, and zucchini in a sizable oven-safe skillet over medium heat until the vegetables are cooked through.
4. When the spinach has wilted, add it to the skillet and cook for an additional 1-2 minutes.
5. Add oregano, basil, and pepper to the vegetables to season.
6. Over the vegetables in the skillet, pour the beaten eggs.
7. The frittata should be baked in the preheated oven for 10 to 12 minutes, or until the top is golden brown and the eggs are set.
8. Slice the frittata and serve it hot.

Macronutrients (per serving): Calories: 220; Carbohydrates: 8g; Protein: 14g; Fat: 15g; Glycemic Index: 20 (low)

Ingredients:

- 4 large eggs
- 1/2 cup chopped onion
- 1/2 cup chopped bell pepper
- 1/2 cup chopped zucchini
- 1/4 cup chopped spinach
- 1 tablespoon olive oil
- Pepper to taste
- 1/4 teaspoon dried basil
- 1/4 teaspoon dried oregano

Berry and Greek Yogurt Parfait

Ingredients:

- 1 cup plain Greek yogurt
- 1/2 cup mixed berries (blueberries, raspberries, strawberries)
- 1 tablespoon chopped walnuts
- 1 tablespoon ground flaxseed
- 1/2 teaspoon vanilla extract
- 1 teaspoon honey

Preparation:
10 Minutes

Servings:
1

Directions:

1. Combine Greek yogurt, vanilla bean paste, and honey in a small bowl.
2. Combine mixed berries and chopped walnuts in another bowl.
3. Layer the yogurt mixture and the berry mixture in a glass or jar.
4. The parfait should be covered with ground flaxseed.
5. Serve right away

Macronutrients (per serving): Calories: 300 Carbohydrates: 23g Protein: 22g Fat: 14g; Glycemic Index: 25 (low)

Sweet Potato Breakfast Bowl

Ingredients:

- 1 large sweet potato, peeled and diced
- 1 tablespoon olive oil
- 1/2 teaspoon ground cinnamon
- 1/2 teaspoon ground nutmeg
- 1/2 cup plain Greek yogurt
- 1/4 cup chopped pecans
- 1 tablespoon honey

Preparation:
20 Minutes

Servings:
2

Directions:

1. Set the oven to 400 °F.
2. Diced sweet potatoes are mixed with olive oil, cinnamon, and nutmeg in a big basin.
3. On a baking sheet, arrange the sweet potatoes in a single layer.
4. Sweet potatoes should be roasted in a preheated oven for 15 to 20 minutes, or until they are soft and slightly caramelized.
5. Combine honey and Greek yogurt in a small bowl.
6. The roasted sweet potatoes should be divided between two bowls.
7. Add a dollop of the Greek yogurt mixture and some chopped pecans to each bowl.
6. Serve right away.

Macronutrients (per serving): Calories: 260; Carbohydrates: 24g; Protein: 7g; Fat: 16g; Glycemic Index: 35 (low)

Veggie Omelet

Ingredients:

- 2 eggs
- 1/4 cup chopped red bell pepper
- 1/4 cup chopped green bell pepper
- 1/4 cup chopped onion
- 1/4 cup chopped mushrooms
- 1 tablespoon olive oil
- Pepper to taste
- 1 slice of whole-grain bread

Preparation:
10 Minutes

Servings:
1

Directions:

1. Whisk the eggs in a bowl, then place it aside.
2. In a nonstick skillet over medium heat, warm the olive oil.
3. Chop the bell peppers, onions, and mushrooms, then add them to the skillet and cook until soft.
4. When the eggs are cooked to the desired doneness, for about 2-3 minutes, pour the whisked eggs into the skillet.
5. With a spatula, carefully fold the omelet in half and cook for an additional 1 to 2 minutes.
6. Along with a piece of whole-grain bread, serve the omelet.

Macronutrients (per serving): 274; Carbs: 13g; Protein: 18g; Fat: 18g; Glycemic Index: 15 (low)

Avocado Toast with Egg

Ingredients:

- 1 slice of whole-grain bread
- 1/2 avocado
- 1 egg
- Pepper to taste
- 1 teaspoon olive oil

Preparation:
10 Minutes

Servings:
1

Directions:

1. The whole-grain bread is toasted.
2. Remove the avocado's pit by halving it. With a fork, mash the avocado in a bowl.
3. Melt the olive oil in a nonstick skillet over medium heat.
4. When the whites are set but the yolk is still runny, crack an egg into a skillet and cook it until it is done.
5. On the toast, spread the mashed avocado and top with pepper.
6. Serve the avocado toast immediately after placing the cooked egg on top of it.

Macronutrients: Calories: 304; Carbs: 19g; Protein: 12g; Fat: 21g; Glycemic Index: 25 (low)

Overnight Oats with Chia Seeds and Berries

Ingredients:

- 1/2 cup rolled oats
- 1 tablespoon chia seeds
- 1/2 cup unsweetened almond milk
- 1/4 cup mixed berries (strawberries, blueberries, raspberries)
- 1 tablespoon honey or maple syrup
- Cinnamon to taste

Preparation:
5 Minutes

Servings:
1

Directions:

1. Mix the rolled oats, chia seeds, almond milk, honey or maple syrup, and cinnamon in a jar or other container with a lid.
2. Stir carefully after adding the mixed berries on top of the oat mixture.
3. Refrigerate overnight with the lid on the jar or container.
4. Stir the oat mixture in the morning, then consume it warm or cold.

Macronutrients: Calories: 326; Carbs: 46g; Protein: 9g; Fat: 11g; Glycemic Index: 35 (low)

Veggie and Cheese Omelette

Ingredients:

- 2 large eggs
- 1/4 cup chopped onion
- 1/4 cup chopped bell pepper
- 1/4 cup chopped tomato
- 1/4 cup shredded low-fat cheddar cheese
- 1 tablespoon olive oil
- Pepper to taste

Preparation:
10 Minutes

Servings:
1

Directions:

1. In a non-stick skillet, heat the olive oil over medium-high heat.
2. When the veggies are tender, add the chopped onion, bell pepper, and tomato to the skillet and simmer for an additional two to three minutes.
3. In a bowl, beat the eggs before adding them to the skillet with vegetables.
4. The eggs should be well cooked after being stirred with a spatula with the vegetables.
5. After topping the omelet with cheese shreds, fold it in half.
6. To taste, add pepper to the dish.

Macronutrients (per serving): Calories: 275; Carbs: 8g; Protein: 21g; Fat: 17g; Glycemic Index: 20 (Low)

Avocado Toast with Turkey Bacon

Ingredients:

- 1 slice of whole-grain bread
- 1/4 avocado
- 2 slices turkey bacon
- 1 small tomato, sliced
- 1 tablespoon olive oil
- Pepper to taste

Preparation:
10 Minutes

Servings:
1

Directions:

1. The whole-grain bread is toasted.
2. With a fork, mash the avocado in a bowl.
3. In a nonstick skillet over medium-high heat, cook the turkey bacon until crispy.
4. On top of the toasted bread, place the tomato slices.
5. Over the tomato slices, spread the mashed avocado.
6. Top the avocado with the cooked turkey bacon.
7. Sprinkle pepper to taste and drizzle olive oil on top.

Macronutrients (per serving): Calories: 315; Carbs: 16g; Protein: 13g; Fat: 22g; Glycemic Index: 15 (Low)

Banana and Peanut Butter Smoothie

Preparation:
50 Minutes

Servings:
2

Directions:

1. The banana should be peeled and chopped.
2. Blend the banana chunks, peanut butter, almond milk, cinnamon, vanilla, and extract.
3. Blend till smooth and creamy at high speed.
4. Serve the smoothie right after pouring it into a glass.

Macronutrients (per serving): Calories: 225; Carbs: 22g; Protein: 7g; Fat: 13g; Glycemic Index: 45 (Low)

Ingredients:

- 1 ripe banana
- 1 tablespoon natural peanut butter
- 1/2 cup unsweetened almond milk
- 1/4 teaspoon vanilla extract
- 1/4 teaspoon cinnamon

Whole Grain Porridge

Ingredients:

- 1/2 cup whole grain oats
- 1 cup unsweetened almond milk
- 1/2 teaspoon cinnamon
- 1 tablespoon chopped nuts (e.g. almonds, pecans)
- 1/2 cup fresh berries (e.g. blueberries, strawberries)
- 1/2 teaspoon stevia or honey (optional)

Preparation:
10 Minutes

Servings:
1

Directions:

1. Oats and almond milk are combined over medium heat in a small pot.
2. Bring the mixture to a boil after adding the cinnamon.
3. Stirring regularly, lower the heat to a simmer for 5 to 7 minutes, or until the oats are cooked and the mixture has thickened.
4. Add the chopped nuts and fresh berries after removing them from the heat.
5. To sweeten the porridge, if desired, add a tiny quantity of stevia or honey.
6. Enjoy warm servings!

Macronutrients (per serving): Calories: 280;
Carbohydrates: 38g; Protein: 9g; Fat: 10g; Glycemic Index: 55

Vegetarian Mains Recipes

Lentil and Vegetable Stir Fry

Preparation:
30 Minutes

Servings:
1

Directions:

1. In a wok or sizable skillet, heat the oil over high heat.
2. Stir-fry the onions, garlic, and ginger for one minute.
3. Add the vegetables and stir-fry for an additional two to three minutes, or until crisp-tender.
4. Stir-fry for a further two minutes after adding the lentils, soy sauce, and black pepper.
5. Add chopped cilantro as a garnish before serving.

Macronutrients (per serving): Calories: 309; Carbs: 42 g; Protein: 16 g; Fat: 8 g; Glycemic Index: 28

Ingredients:

- 1/2 cup cooked lentils
- 1/2 cup mixed vegetables (broccoli, carrots, snow peas, bell pepper)
- 1/4 cup sliced onions
- 1 tsp minced garlic
- 1 tsp minced ginger
- 1 tbsp olive oil
- 1 tbsp low-sodium soy sauce
- 1/4 tsp ground black pepper
- 1 tbsp chopped fresh cilantro

Quinoa and Vegetable Salad

Ingredients:

- 1/2 cup cooked quinoa
- 1/2 cup mixed vegetables (tomatoes, cucumbers, bell pepper, onion)
- 1 tbsp chopped fresh parsley
- 1 tbsp chopped fresh mint
- 1 tbsp chopped fresh basil
- 1 tbsp lemon juice
- 1 tbsp olive oil
- 1 tsp honey
- 1/4 tsp ground black pepper

Preparation:
20 Minutes

Servings:
1

Directions:

1. In a bowl, mix the quinoa, veggies, parsley, mint, and basil.
2. Whisk the lemon juice, olive oil, honey, and black pepper in a separate bowl.
3. Toss the quinoa mixture with the dressing after pouring it over it.
4. Serving suggestions: Cool or room temperature.

Macronutrients (per serving): Calories: 328; Carbs: 45 g; Protein: 9 g; Fat: 14 g; Glycemic Index: 53

Chickpea and Spinach Curry

Ingredients:

- 1/2 cup cooked chickpeas
- 1 cup fresh spinach
- 1/4 cup chopped onion
- 1 tsp minced garlic
- 1 tsp minced ginger
- 1/4 cup diced tomatoes
- 1 tsp curry powder
- 1/4 tsp ground cumin
- 1/4 tsp ground coriander
- 1/4 tsp ground turmeric
- 1 tbsp olive oil
- 1/4 cup water
- 1 tbsp chopped fresh cilantro

Preparation:
30 Minutes

Servings:
1

Directions:

1. In a pan over medium heat, warm the oil.
2. When the onions are transparent, add the ginger, garlic, and onions.
3. Cook for one minute after adding the tomatoes, curry powder, cumin, coriander, and turmeric.
4. After adding the spinach and water, boil the mixture for 10 minutes.
5. Add chopped cilantro as a garnish before serving.

Macronutrients (per serving): Calories: 316; Carbs: 43 g; Protein: 11 g; Fat: 12 g; Glycemic Index: 32

Broccoli and Mushroom Stir-Fry

Preparation:
25 Minutes

Servings:
1

Directions:

1. In a wok or sizable skillet, heat the oil over high heat.
2. Stir-fry the onions, garlic, and ginger for one minute.
3. Stir-fry the broccoli and mushrooms for two to three minutes, or until they are crisp-tender.
4. Stir-fry for an additional two minutes after adding the soy sauce and black pepper.
5. Add chopped parsley as a garnish before serving.

Macronutrients (per serving): Calories: 208; Carbs: 14 g; Protein: 7 g; Fat: 15 g; Glycemic Index: 15

Ingredients:

- 1 cup broccoli florets
- 1 cup sliced mushrooms
- 1/4 cup sliced onions
- 1 tsp minced garlic
- 1 tsp minced ginger
- 1 tbsp olive oil
- 1 tbsp low-sodium soy sauce
- 1/4 tsp ground black pepper
- 1 tbsp chopped fresh parsley

Zucchini and Red Pepper Frittata

Ingredients:

- 1/2 cup sliced zucchini
- 1/4 cup diced red bell pepper
- 1/4 cup diced onion
- 2 eggs
- 1/4 cup of low-fat milk
- 1/4 tsp dried basil
- 1/4 tsp dried oregano
- 1/4 tsp garlic powder
- 1 tbsp olive oil

Preparation:
30 Minutes

Servings:
2

Directions:

1. Set the oven's temperature to 350°F (180°C).
2. In a small oven-safe skillet, heat the oil over medium heat.
3. When the onion, bell pepper, and zucchini are added, sauté them until they are soft.
4. Beat the eggs, milk, basil, oregano, and garlic powder together in a small bowl.
5. Over the veggies in the skillet, pour the egg mixture.
6. Bake the eggs for 15 to 20 minutes, or until they are done.
7. Serve warm.

Macronutrients (per serving): Calories: 298; Carbs: 12 g; Protein: 15 g; Fat: 22 g; Glycemic Index: 25

Cauliflower Rice and Black Bean Bowl

Ingredients:

- 1 cup cauliflower rice
- 1/2 cup cooked black beans
- 1/4 cup diced tomatoes
- 1/4 cup diced red onion
- 1 tbsp chopped fresh cilantro
- 1 tbsp lime juice
- 1 tbsp olive oil
- 1/4 tsp ground cumin
- 1/4 tsp chili powder
- 1/4 tsp garlic powder

Preparation:
30 Minutes

Servings:
1

Directions:

1. In a skillet over medium heat, warm the oil.
2. Cauliflower rice should be added and cooked for 3 to 4 minutes, or until soft.
3. Cook the red onion, tomatoes, and black beans for an additional two to three minutes.
4. Stir in the cumin, lime juice, chili powder, garlic powder, cilantro, and cumin to mix.
5. Serve warm.

Macronutrients (per serving): Calories: 334; Carbs: 40 g; Protein: 13 g; Fat: 14 g; Glycemic Index: 30

Sweet Potato Breakfast Bowl

Preparation:
40 Minutes

Servings:
1

Directions:

1. The lentils should be rinsed before soaking for 20 minutes.
2. In a big pot, warm the oil over medium heat.
3. For two to three minutes, add the onions, garlic, and ginger.
4. For an additional 5 minutes, add the bell peppers, potatoes, and carrots.
5. Add the lentils to the pot after draining them.
6. Add the cumin, coriander, turmeric, cayenne pepper, and black pepper along with the veggie broth.
7. When the lentils and vegetables are cooked, simmer for 20 to 25 minutes after bringing them to a boil.
8. Serve hot and garnish with chopped cilantro.

Macronutrients (per serving): Calories: 429; Carbs: 68 g; Protein: 20 g; Fat: 9 g; Glycemic Index: 28

Ingredients:

- 1/2 cup dry red lentils
- 1/2 cup diced carrots
- 1/2 cup diced potatoes
- 1/2 cup diced onions
- 1/2 cup diced bell peppers
- 1 tsp minced garlic
- 1 tsp minced ginger
- 1 tbsp olive oil
- 1/4 cup low-sodium vegetable broth
- 1/2 tsp ground cumin
- 1/2 tsp ground coriander
- 1/2 tsp turmeric
- 1/4 tsp cayenne pepper
- 1/4 tsp ground black pepper
- 1 tbsp chopped fresh cilantro

Spinach and Tofu Stir-Fry

Ingredients:

- 1 cup chopped spinach
- 1/2 cup cubed tofu
- 1/2 cup sliced mushrooms
- 1/4 cup sliced onions
- 1 tsp minced garlic
- 1 tsp minced ginger
- 1 tbsp olive oil
- 1 tbsp low-sodium soy sauce
- 1/4 tsp ground black pepper
- 1 tbsp chopped fresh cilantro

Preparation:
30 Minutes

Servings:
1

Directions:

1. In a wok or sizable skillet, heat the oil over high heat.
2. Stir-fry the onions, garlic, and ginger for one minute.
3. Stir-fry the mushrooms for two to three minutes, or until they are soft.
4. When the spinach has wilted and the tofu is well cooked, add the tofu and spinach and stir-fry for an additional 2 to 3 minutes.
5. Stir in the black pepper and soy sauce after adding them.
6. Serve hot and garnish with chopped cilantro.

Macronutrients (per serving): Calories: 296; Carbs: 11 g; Protein: 18 g; Fat: 21 g; Glycemic Index: 15

Sweet Potato Breakfast Bowl

Ingredients:

- 1/2 cup cooked chickpeas
- 1/2 cup diced carrots
- 1/2 cup diced celery
- 1/2 cup diced onions
- 1/2 cup diced tomatoes
- 1 tsp minced garlic
- 1 tsp minced ginger
- 1 tbsp olive oil
- 1/4 cup low-sodium vegetable broth
- 1/2 tsp ground cumin
- 1/2 tsp ground coriander
- 1/4 tsp turmeric
- 1/4 tsp ground black pepper
- 1 tbsp chopped fresh parsley

Preparation:
45 Minutes

Servings:
1

Directions:

1. In a big pot, warm the oil over medium heat.
2. For two to three minutes, add the onions, garlic, and ginger.
3. For an additional five minutes, add the carrots and celery and continue to sauté.
4. Add the black pepper, turmeric, cumin, coriander, tomatoes, chickpeas, and vegetable broth.
5. Once the mixture has come to a boil, turn down the heat, cover, and simmer for 25–30 minutes, or until the veggies are soft.
6. Serve hot and garnish with parsley.

Macronutrients (per serving): Calories: 353; Carbs: 52 g; Protein: 13 g; Fat: 12 g; Glycemic Index: 32

Lentil and Vegetable Stew

Ingredients:

- 1/2 cup dried green lentils
- 1/2 cup diced carrots
- 1/2 cup diced celery
- 1/2 cup diced onion
- 2 cloves garlic, minced
- 1/2 cup diced tomatoes
- 2 cups vegetable broth
- 1 tsp ground cumin
- 1 tsp paprika
- 1/4 tsp ground black pepper
- 1 tbsp chopped fresh parsley

Preparation:
40 Minutes

Servings:
1

Directions:

1. After thoroughly washing them, add the lentils to a big pot and cover them with an inch of water. Over high heat, bring to a boil; then, turn down the heat and simmer for 15 to 20 minutes, or until soft. Drain, then set apart.
2. A little oil should be heated on medium heat in the same saucepan. When the vegetables are soft, add the carrots, celery, onion, and garlic and sauté for 5-7 minutes.
3. To the pot, add the tomatoes, veggie broth, cumin, paprika, and black pepper. To blend, stir.
4. Bring to a boil, then lower the heat and simmer for 15 to 20 minutes, depending on how tender you like your vegetables.
5. Stir in the cooked lentils after adding them to the pot. To fully reheat, simmer for an additional five minutes.
6. Serve hot and garnish with parsley.

Macronutrients (per serving): Calories: 314; Carbs: 54 g; Protein: 19 g; Fat: 2 g; Glycemic Index: 33

Grains, Beans, and Legumes Recipes

Quinoa Salad with Chickpeas and Vegetables

Preparation:
20 Minutes

Servings:
1

Directions:

1. Combine the quinoa, chickpeas, cucumber, red bell pepper, and red onion in a mixing bowl.
2. Combine the olive oil, lemon juice, parsley, and black pepper in a different bowl.
3. Toss the quinoa mixture with the dressing after pouring it over it.
4. Serve right now or keep chilled until you're ready to dine.

Macronutrients (per serving): Calories: 350; Carbs: 46g; Protein: 12g; Fat: 14g; Glycemic Index: 53

Ingredients:

- 1/2 cup cooked quinoa
- 1/2 cup canned chickpeas, drained and rinsed
- 1/4 cup chopped cucumber
- 1/4 cup chopped red bell pepper
- 1/4 cup chopped red onion
- 1 tablespoon olive oil
- 1 tablespoon lemon juice
- 1 tablespoon chopped fresh parsley
- 1/4 teaspoon black pepper

Lentil Soup with Vegetables

Ingredients:

- 1/2 cup dried lentils
- 1/4 cup chopped onion
- 1/4 cup chopped carrot
- 1/4 cup chopped celery
- 1 clove garlic, minced
- 1 tablespoon olive oil
- 2 cups water
- 1 bay leaf
- 1/4 teaspoon black pepper
- 1/4 teaspoon cumin

Preparation:
30 Minutes

Servings:
1

Directions:

1. In a sieve, rinse the lentils and set them aside.
2. Olive oil should be used to sauté the onion, carrot, celery, and garlic in a pot until tender.
3. To the pot, add the lentils, water, bay leaf, cumin, and black pepper.
4. The mixture should be brought to a boil, then simmered for 20 to 25 minutes, or until the lentils are cooked.
5. Remove and discard the bay leaf.
6. Serve right away.

Macronutrients (per serving): Calories: 340; Carbs: 51g; Protein: 20g; Fat: 6g; Glycemic Index: 28

Brown Rice and Vegetable Stir-Fry

Ingredients:

- 1/2 cup cooked brown rice
- 1/4 cup chopped onion
- 1/4 cup chopped red bell pepper
- 1/4 cup chopped zucchini
- 1/4 cup chopped broccoli
- 1 tablespoon olive oil
- 1 clove garlic, minced
- 1/4 teaspoon black pepper
- 1/4 teaspoon ginger

Preparation: 30 Minutes

Servings: 1

Directions:

1. Olive oil should be used to cook the onion, red bell pepper, zucchini, and broccoli in a pan until they are soft.
2. Stir together the ginger, garlic, and black pepper in the pan after adding them.
3. Stir in the brown rice after it has been cooked in the pan.
4. Serve right away.

Macronutrients (per serving): Calories: 320; Carbs: 46g; Protein: 7g; Fat: 13g; Glycemic Index: 50

Quinoa and Black Bean Salad

Ingredients:

- 1/2 cup cooked quinoa
- 1/2 cup canned black beans, rinsed and drained
- 1/4 cup diced tomatoes
- 1/4 cup diced bell pepper
- 1/4 cup diced cucumber
- 2 tablespoons chopped cilantro
- 1 tablespoon olive oil
- 1 tablespoon freshly squeezed lime juice
- 1/4 teaspoon ground cumin
- 1/4 teaspoon chili powder
- Salt and pepper to taste

Preparation: 15 Minutes

Servings: 1

Directions:

1. Quinoa, black beans, tomatoes, bell pepper, cucumber, and cilantro should all be combined in a big bowl.
2. Mix the olive oil, lime juice, cumin, and chili powder in another bowl.
3. Toss the quinoa mixture with the dressing after pouring it over it.
4. To taste, add salt and pepper to the food.
5. Serve right away or keep chilled until you're ready to.

Macronutrients (per serving): Calories: 348; Carbs: 46g; Protein: 12g; Fat: 13g; Glycemic Index: 53

Brown Rice and Vegetable Stir-Fry

Preparation:
30 Minutes

Servings:
1

Directions:

1. Olive oil should be heated in a sizable skillet over medium heat.
2. Saute the onions and garlic till transparent after adding them.
3. Cook the sweet potatoes after being added until just barely soft.
4. Stir to mix the chickpeas, cumin, coriander, turmeric, paprika, and cinnamon in the skillet.
5. Stir together the veggie broth and diced tomatoes from a can in the skillet.
6. Once the mixture has come to a boil, turn down the heat and let it simmer for 15 to 20 minutes, or until the sweet potatoes are fork-tender and the flavors are well-balanced.
7. To taste, add salt and pepper to the food.
8. Combined with heated brown rice.

Macronutrients (per serving): Calories: 413; Carbs: 63g; Protein: 12g; Fat: 13g; Glycemic Index: 41

Ingredients:

- 1/2 cup canned chickpeas, rinsed and drained
- 1/2 cup cubed sweet potato
- 1/4 cup chopped onion
- 1 garlic clove, minced
- 1 tablespoon olive oil
- 1/2 teaspoon ground cumin
- 1/2 teaspoon ground coriander
- 1/4 teaspoon turmeric
- 1/4 teaspoon paprika
- 1/4 teaspoon cinnamon
- 1/2 cup canned diced tomatoes
- 1/2 cup low-sodium vegetable broth
- Salt and pepper to taste

Quinoa and Vegetable Stir-Fry

Ingredients:

- 1/2 cup cooked quinoa
- 1/2 cup chopped broccoli
- 1/2 cup chopped carrots
- 1/2 cup chopped bell pepper
- 1/4 cup chopped onion
- 1 garlic clove, minced
- 1 tablespoon olive oil
- 1/4 teaspoon ground ginger
- 1/4 teaspoon ground cumin
- 1/4 teaspoon paprika
- 1/4 teaspoon turmeric
- 1 tablespoon low-sodium soy sauce

Preparation: 20 Minutes

Servings: 1

Directions:

1. Olive oil should be heated to a medium-high temperature in a big skillet.
2. Saute the onions and garlic till transparent after adding them.
3. Cook until soft after including the bell pepper, broccoli, and carrots.
4. Stir in the ground ginger, cumin, paprika, and turmeric after adding them to the skillet.
5. Stir the cooked quinoa into the skillet after adding it.
6. Stir in the soy sauce after adding it.
7. To enable the flavors to mingle, cook for a further 1-2 minutes.
8. Serve warm.

Macronutrients (per serving): Calories: 337; Carbs: 56g; Protein: 10g; Fat: 9g; Glycemic Index: 53

Lentil and Spinach Soup

Ingredients:

- 1/2 cup dried lentils, rinsed and drained
- 1 cup chopped spinach
- 1/4 cup chopped onion
- 1 garlic clove, minced
- 1 tablespoon olive oil
- 1 bay leaf
- 1/4 teaspoon dried thyme
- 2 cups low-sodium vegetable broth
- Salt and pepper to taste

Preparation: 30 Minutes

Servings: 1

Directions:

1. Olive oil should be heated in a sizable pot over medium-high heat.
2. Saute the onions and garlic till transparent after adding them.
3. Stir together the dried lentils, vegetable broth, bay leaf, and thyme in the pot.
4. Bring to a boil, then lower the heat and simmer the lentils for 20 to 25 minutes, or until they are cooked through.
5. Stir in the chopped spinach after adding it to the pot.
6. Cook the spinach for a further 3-5 minutes, or until it has wilted.
7. To taste, add salt and pepper to the food.
8. Serve warm.

Macronutrients (per serving): Calories: 285; Carbs: 43g; Protein: 19g; Fat: 4g; Glycemic Index: 28

Black Bean and Vegetable Soup

Preparation:
30 Minutes

Servings:
1

Directions:

1. Olive oil should be heated in a sizable pot over medium-high heat.
2. Saute the onions and garlic till transparent after adding them.
3. Once the carrots and celery are soft, add them.
4. Stir together the vegetable broth, canned diced tomatoes, canned black beans, bay leaf, and thyme in the pot.
5. Once the mixture has come to a boil, turn down the heat, cover, and simmer for 15 to 20 minutes, or until the veggies are soft.
6. To taste, add salt and pepper to the food.
7. Serve warm.

Macronutrients (per serving): Calories: 253; Carbs: 38g; Protein: 12g; Fat: 7g; Glycemic Index: 41

Ingredients:

- 1/2 cup canned black beans, rinsed and drained
- 1/2 cup chopped carrots
- 1/2 cup chopped celery
- 1/4 cup chopped onion
- 1 garlic clove, minced
- 1 tablespoon olive oil
- 1 bay leaf
- 1/4 teaspoon dried thyme
- 2 cups low-sodium vegetable broth
- 1/2 cup canned diced tomatoes
- Salt and pepper to taste

Lentil and Spinach Soup

Ingredients:

- 1/2 cup dried lentils, rinsed and drained
- 1 cup chopped spinach
- 1/4 cup chopped onion
- 1 garlic clove, minced
- 1 tablespoon olive oil
- 1 bay leaf
- 1/4 teaspoon dried thyme
- 2 cups low-sodium vegetable broth
- Salt and pepper to taste

Preparation:
30 Minutes

Servings:
1

Directions:

9. Olive oil should be heated in a sizable pot over medium-high heat.
10. Saute the onions and garlic till transparent after adding them.
11. Stir together the dried lentils, vegetable broth, bay leaf, and thyme in the pot.
12. Bring to a boil, then lower the heat and simmer the lentils for 20 to 25 minutes, or until they are cooked through.
13. Stir in the chopped spinach after adding it to the pot.
14. Cook the spinach for a further 3-5 minutes, or until it has wilted.
15. To taste, add salt and pepper to the food.
16. Serve warm.

Macronutrients (per serving): Calories: 285; Carbs: 43g; Protein: 19g; Fat: 4g; Glycemic Index: 28

Brown Rice and Bean Burrito Bowl

Ingredients:

- 1 cup cooked brown rice
- 1 can black beans, rinsed and drained
- 1 small red bell pepper, chopped
- 1 small avocado, diced
- 1/4 cup chopped fresh cilantro
- 2 tablespoons lime juice
- 1 tablespoon olive oil
- Salt and pepper, to taste

Preparation:
25 Minutes

Servings:
2

Directions:

1. Cooked brown rice, black beans, diced avocado, red bell pepper, and fresh cilantro should all be combined in a big bowl.
2. Mix the lime juice, olive oil, salt, and pepper in a small bowl.
3. Mix the rice and bean mixture with the dressing after pouring it over them.
4. Serve right away.

Macronutrients (per serving): Calories: 438; Carbs: 60g; Protein: 12g; Fat: 19g; Glycemic Index: 50

Spicy Chickpea and Spinach Curry

Ingredients:

- 1/2 cup cooked chickpeas
- 1/2 cup chopped spinach
- 1/4 cup diced tomatoes
- 1/4 cup chopped onion
- 1 clove minced garlic
- 1/2 teaspoon grated ginger
- 1/2 teaspoon ground cumin
- 1/2 teaspoon ground coriander
- 1/4 teaspoon turmeric
- 1/4 teaspoon cayenne pepper
- 1/2 cup water
- 1 teaspoon olive oil
- 1 teaspoon honey or stevia (optional)

Preparation:
30 Minutes

Servings:
1

Directions:

1. In a small saucepan over medium heat, warm the olive oil.
2. When the onion is soft and transparent, add it and cook for 3–4 minutes.
3. Cook for a further minute after adding the garlic and ginger.
4. While constantly stirring, add the cumin, coriander, turmeric, and cayenne pepper. Cook for 1-2 minutes.
5. Bring to a boil the chickpeas, water, and diced tomatoes.
6. Once the sauce has thickened and the chickpeas are well heated, turn the heat down to low and allow the mixture to simmer for 10 to 15 minutes.
7. Add the spinach and simmer for an additional 2 to 3 minutes, or until wilted.
8. With a sprinkle of honey or stevia, if preferred, remove from heat and serve immediately.

Macronutrients (per serving): Calories: 292 Carbs: 47g; Protein: 13g; Fat: 6g; Glycemic Index: 28

Beef, Pork, and Lamb Recipes

Beef Stir-Fry

Ingredients:

- 3 oz lean beef, sliced into thin strips
- 1 cup mixed vegetables (broccoli, bell pepper, onion, carrot)
- 1 tbsp olive oil
- 1 garlic clove, minced
- 1 tsp ginger, grated
- 1 tbsp low-sodium soy sauce
- 1/2 tsp honey
- 1/2 cup cooked brown rice

Preparation:
20 Minutes

Servings:
1

Directions:

1. In a wok or sizable skillet, heat the oil over high heat.
2. Stir-fry the steak after adding it until both sides are browned.
3. Stir-fry the garlic and ginger for 30 seconds after adding them.
4. Stir-fry the veggies for 2–3 minutes, or until crisp–tender, after adding them.
5. Soy sauce and honey should be blended together in a small bowl. Stir-fry for an additional 1-2 minutes after adding to the pan.
6. the stir-fry over brown rice that has been cooked.

Macronutrients (per serving): Calories: 390; Carbs: 39g; Protein: 29g; Fat: 13g; Glycemic Index: 50

Brown Rice and Vegetable Stir-Fry

Preparation:
25 Minutes

Servings:
1

Directions:

1. In a big skillet over medium-high heat, warm the oil.
2. Salt and pepper the pork chop before adding it to the skillet. Cook for 3 to 4 minutes on each side, or until well done.
3. The pork chop should be taken out of the griddle and placed aside.
4. To the skillet, add the chopped apple and onion, and cook for 3–4 minutes, or until soft.
5. Combine the apple cider vinegar, honey, cinnamon, and ginger in a small bowl. Add to the skillet and stir continuously for an additional 1-2 minutes of cooking.
6. Serve the pork chop with the apple chutney on top and some cooked quinoa on the side.

Macronutrients (per serving): Calories: 390; Carbs: 45g; Protein: 29g; Fat: 10g; Glycemic Index: 53

Ingredients:

- 1 boneless pork chop (4 oz)
- 1 tsp olive oil
- 1/2 cup chopped apple
- 1/4 cup chopped onion
- 1 tbsp apple cider vinegar
- 1/2 tsp honey
- 1/4 tsp ground cinnamon
- 1/4 tsp ground ginger
- 1/4 cup cooked quinoa

Herb-Roasted Chicken Thighs

Ingredients:

- 2 boneless chicken thighs (4 oz)
- 1 tsp olive oil
- 1/2 tsp dried thyme
- 1/2 tsp dried rosemary
- 1/2 tsp garlic powder
- 1/4 tsp black pepper
- 1 cup chopped vegetables (carrots, Brussels sprouts, onion)
- 1/4 cup cooked quinoa

Preparation: 40 Minutes

Servings: 1

Directions:

1. Set the oven to 400°F.
2. Combine the thyme, rosemary, garlic powder, and black pepper in a small bowl.
3. Rub the olive oil all over the chicken thighs before placing them in a baking dish.
4. To evenly coat the chicken thighs, sprinkle the herb mixture over them and give them a good rubdown.
5. Around the chicken in the baking dish, arrange the finely chopped vegetables.
6. Roast in the oven for 25 to 30 minutes, or until the veggies are soft and the chicken is thoroughly cooked.
7. Along with the roasted chicken thighs and vegetables, serve cooked quinoa as a side dish.

Macronutrients (per serving): Calories: 450; Carbs: 34g; Protein: 36g; Fat: 18g; Glycemic Index: 35

Grilled Pork Tenderloin with Peach Salsa

Preparation: 30 Minutes

Servings: 1

Ingredients:

- 4 oz pork tenderloin
- 1 tsp olive oil
- 1/2 tsp smoked paprika
- 1/4 tsp garlic powder
- 1/2 cup diced peaches
- 1/4 cup diced red onion
- 1/4 cup chopped fresh cilantro
- 1 tbsp lime juice
- 1/4 tsp honey
- 1/2 cup cooked quinoa

Directions:

1. Grill or grill pan should be heated to medium-high.
2. Garlic powder, smoked paprika, and olive oil are rubbed onto the pork tenderloin.
3. Pork tenderloin should be cooked thoroughly on the grill for 3 to 4 minutes on each side.
4. Make the salsa while the pork is cooking: Combine the chopped peaches, red onion, cilantro, lime juice, and honey in a small bowl.
5. With a side of cooked quinoa, serve the pork tenderloin topped with peach salsa.

Macronutrients (per serving): Calories: 400; Carbs: 35g; Protein: 30g; Fat: 16g; Glycemic Index: 53

Baked Salmon with Roasted Vegetables

Preparation:
30 Minutes

Servings:
1

Ingredients:

- 4 oz salmon fillet
- 1 tsp olive oil
- 1/4 tsp garlic powder
- 1/4 tsp smoked paprika
- 1/2 cup chopped vegetables (zucchini, bell pepper, onion, carrot)
- 1 tsp olive oil
- 1/4 tsp dried oregano
- 1/4 tsp dried thyme
- 1/4 tsp black pepper
- 1/2 cup cooked quinoa

Directions:

1. Set the oven to 400°F.
2. Garlic powder, smoked paprika, and olive oil should be applied to the salmon fillet.
3. On a baking sheet, place the salmon fillet, and bake for 12 to 15 minutes, or until done.
4. Toss the chopped veggies with olive oil, oregano, thyme, and black pepper while the fish is cooking. They should be spread out on a different baking sheet and baked for 15 to 20 minutes, or until soft.
5. Serve cooked quinoa on the side with baked salmon and roasted vegetables.

Macronutrients (per serving): Calories: 450; Carbs: 33g; Protein: 34g; Fat: 20g; Glycemic Index: 53

Turkey and Black Bean Chili

Ingredients:

- 3 oz ground turkey
- 1 tsp olive oil
- 1/4 cup chopped onion
- 1/4 cup chopped bell pepper
- 1 garlic clove, minced
- 1/2 cup low-sodium canned black beans, drained and rinsed
- 1/2 cup canned diced tomatoes
- 1/2 cup low-sodium chicken broth
- 1/2 tsp chili powder
- 1/4 tsp ground cumin
- 1/4 tsp smoked paprika
- 1/4 cup chopped fresh cilantro
- 1/4 avocado, diced

Preparation:
45 Minutes

Servings:
1

Directions:

1. In a medium saucepan set over medium heat, warm the olive oil.
2. Add the ground turkey and simmer for 5-7 minutes, or until browned, while stirring regularly. 3. Add the minced garlic, chopped onion, and bell pepper to the pan and cook for 2 to 3 minutes, or until the veggies are soft.
3. To the saucepan, add the rinsed and drained black beans, chopped tomatoes, chicken broth, cumin, and smoked paprika. To blend, stir.
4. For 20 to 25 minutes, or when the flavors have combined and the chili has thickened, bring the chili to a simmer.
5. Add the chopped cilantro and stir.
6. Top the turkey and black bean chili with cubed avocado before serving.

Macronutrients (per serving): Calories: 350; Carbs: 27g; Protein: 28g; Fat: 15g; Glycemic Index: 45

Grilled Flank Steak with Chimichurri Sauce

Ingredients:

- 4 oz flank steak
- 1 tsp olive oil
- 1/2 tsp smoked paprika
- 1/4 tsp garlic powder
- 1/2 cup fresh parsley leaves
- 1/4 cup fresh cilantro leaves
- 1 garlic clove, minced
- 1 tbsp red wine vinegar
- 1/2 tsp honey
- 1/4 tsp red pepper flakes
- 1/2 cup cooked brown rice

Preparation:
40 Minutes

Servings:
1

Directions:

1. Grill or grill pan should be heated to medium-high.
2. Garlic powder, smoked paprika, and olive oil should be applied to the flank steak.
3. Grill the flank steak for 3 to 4 minutes on each side, depending on how done you like it.
4. Make the chimichurri sauce while the steak cooks. Combine the parsley, cilantro, garlic, red wine vinegar, honey, and red pepper flakes in a small food processor or blender. Pulse several times to thoroughly incorporate the ingredients and cut the herbs.
5. Along with a side of cooked brown rice, serve the grilled flank steak with the chimichurri sauce.

Macronutrients (per serving): Calories: 450; Carbs: 30g; Protein: 34g; Fat: 22g; Glycemic Index: 50

Roasted Pork Loin with Apple and Onion

Ingredients:

- 4 oz pork loin
- 1 tsp olive oil
- 1/4 tsp dried thyme
- 1/4 tsp smoked paprika
- 1/2 cup chopped apple
- 1/4 cup chopped red onion
- 1 tbsp balsamic vinegar
- 1/2 cup cooked quinoa

Preparation:
45 Minutes

Servings:
1

Directions:

1. To 400°F, preheat the oven.
2. The olive oil, dried thyme, and smoked paprika should be applied to the pork loin.
3. Roast the pork loin for 20 to 25 minutes, or until it is thoroughly cooked, on a baking sheet.
4. Toss the apple and red onion with the balsamic vinegar while the pork is cooking. They should be spread out on a different baking sheet and baked for 10 to 15 minutes, or until soft.
5. With a side of cooked quinoa, serve the roasted pork loin with an apple and onion mixture.

Macronutrients (per serving): Calories: 450; Carbs: 35g; Protein: 36g; Fat: 18g; Glycemic Index: 45

Brown Rice and Vegetable Stir-Fry

Ingredients:

- 3 oz ground turkey
- 1 tsp olive oil
- 1/4 cup sliced bell pepper
- 1/4 cup sliced zucchini
- 1/4 cup sliced onion
- 1 garlic clove, minced
- 1 tbsp low-sodium soy sauce
- 1 tsp honey
- 1/2 cup cooked brown rice

Preparation:
30 Minutes

Servings:
1

Directions:

1. In a wok or sizable skillet, heat the olive oil over high heat.
2. Add the ground turkey and cook for 3–4 minutes, stirring often, or until browned.
3. To the wok or skillet, add the thinly sliced bell pepper, zucchini, onion, and minced garlic. Vegetables should be stir-fried for 3–4 minutes, or until they are crisp-tender. 4. Mix the honey and low-sodium soy sauce in a small bowl.
4. The turkey and veggies in the wok or skillet should be covered with the soy sauce mixture. Stir-fry for a further 1-2 minutes, or until the sauce has been well distributed throughout.
5. Over a bed of cooked brown rice, plate the stir-fry with the turkey and vegetables.

Macronutrients (per serving): Calories: 360; Carbs: 39g; Protein: 22g; Fat: 12g; Glycemic Index: 55

Lemon and Herb Roasted Chicken

Ingredients:

- 4 oz boneless, skinless chicken breast
- 1 tsp olive oil
- 1 garlic clove, minced
- 1 tbsp fresh lemon juice
- 1/4 tsp dried oregano
- 1/4 tsp dried thyme
- 1/2 cup roasted Brussels sprouts
- 1/2 cup roasted sweet potato

Preparation:
50 Minutes

Servings:
1

Directions:

1. Set the oven to 400°F.
2. Olive oil, minced garlic, lemon juice, dried oregano, and dried thyme should be applied to the chicken breast.
3. A baking sheet should be used to roast the chicken breast for 25 to 30 minutes, or until it is thoroughly done.
4. Roast the sweet potato and Brussels sprouts on a different baking sheet in the oven for 20 to 25 minutes, or until they are fork-tender and lightly browned, while the chicken is cooking.
5. Serve roasted chicken with lemon and herbs alongside roasted sweet potato and Brussels sprouts.

Macronutrients (per serving): Calories: 400; Carbs: 34g; Protein: 34g; Fat: 14g; Glycemic Index: 50

Fish and seafood Recipes

Garlic and Herb Shrimp Skewers

Ingredients:

- 8 large raw shrimp, peeled and deveined
- 1 tablespoon olive oil
- 1 clove garlic, minced
- 1 teaspoon dried basil
- 1 teaspoon dried oregano
- 1/4 teaspoon black pepper
- 1/4 teaspoon paprika
- 1/4 teaspoon cayenne pepper
- 1 lemon, cut into wedges

Preparation:
20 Minutes

Servings:
1

Directions:

1. Olive oil, garlic, basil, oregano, black pepper, paprika, and cayenne pepper should all be combined in a small bowl. Mix thoroughly.
2. Thread shrimp onto skewers.
3. Apply the herb mixture to the shrimp.
4. To medium-high heat, place a grill or grill pan.
5. The shrimp should be cooked through and pink on the grill for 2-3 minutes on each side.
6. Lemon wedges should be served on the side.

Macronutrients (per serving): Calories: 155; Carbs: 2g; Protein: 22g; Fat: 7g; Glycemic Index: 0

Baked Lemon Salmon with Asparagus

Ingredients:

- 4 oz salmon fillet
- 1/2 lemon, sliced
- 5 spears of asparagus, trimmed
- 1/2 tablespoon olive oil
- 1 clove garlic, minced
- 1/4 teaspoon black pepper
- 1/4 teaspoon dried thyme
- 1/4 teaspoon dried rosemary
- 1/4 teaspoon dried parsley

Preparation:
25 Minutes

Servings:
1

Directions:

1. Set the oven's temperature to 400°F (200°C).
2. The center of a baking dish should include the salmon fillet.
3. Place the salmon in the middle of the asparagus.
4. Olive oil, garlic, black pepper, thyme, rosemary, and parsley should all be combined in a small bowl. the fish and asparagus with a drizzle.
5. Lemon slices should be placed on top of the salmon.
6. Bake the salmon for 15 to 20 minutes, or until it is done.
7. Serve warm.

Macronutrients (per serving): Calories: 266; Carbs: 7g; Protein: 27g; Fat: 15g; Glycemic Index: 0

Grilled Tuna Salad

Preparation:
20 Minutes

Servings:
1

Directions:

1. Preheat the grill or grill pan to medium-high heat.
2. Apply olive oil to the tuna steak and season with basil, oregano, and black pepper.
3. Grill the tuna until well cooked, about 2 to 3 minutes per side.
4. Salad greens, cherry tomatoes, cucumber, and red onion should all be combined in a big bowl.
5. Mix the olive oil and balsamic vinegar in a small basin.
6. Toss the salad with the dressing after pouring it over it.
7. Add the sliced tuna to the salad.
8. Serve right away.

Macronutrients (per serving): Calories: 254; Carbs: 9g; Protein: 29g; Fat: 12g; Glycemic Index: 20

Ingredients:

- 4 oz tuna steak
- 2 cups mixed salad greens
- 1/2 cup cherry tomatoes, halved
- 1/4 cup cucumber, sliced
- 1/4 cup red onion, sliced
- 1/2 tablespoon olive oil
- 1/2 tablespoon balsamic vinegar
- 1/4 teaspoon black pepper
- 1/4 teaspoon dried oregano
- 1/4 teaspoon dried basil

Pan-Seared Scallops with Roasted Vegetables

Ingredients:

- 4 large scallops
- 1/2 tablespoon olive oil
- 1/2 tablespoon unsalted butter
- 1 clove garlic, minced
- 1/4 teaspoon black pepper
- 1/4 teaspoon dried thyme
- 1/4 teaspoon dried basil
- 1/2 cup Brussels sprouts, halved
- 1/2 cup carrots, sliced
- 1/2 cup red bell pepper, sliced

Preparation:
30 Minutes

Servings:
1

Directions:

1. Set the oven's temperature to 400°F (200°C).
2. Combine Brussels sprouts, carrots, and red bell pepper in a big bowl with a tablespoon of olive oil. On a baking sheet, arrange the vegetables in a single layer and roast for 15-20 minutes, or until soft.
3. Combine the butter, basil, thyme, garlic, and black pepper in a small bowl.
4. Scallops should be dried with a paper towel.
5. A nonstick skillet should be heated to medium-high.
6. Scallops should be added to the skillet and cooked for two to three minutes on each side until golden.
7. Swish the scallops in the butter mixture after adding them to the skillet.
8. Serve roasted vegetables beside the scallops.

Macronutrients (per serving): Calories: 234; Carbs: 17g; Protein: 17g; Fat: 12g; Glycemic Index: 0

Tuna Avocado Lettuce Wraps

Ingredients:

- 4 oz canned tuna, drained
- 1/4 avocado, mashed
- 2 leaves butter lettuce
- 1/4 cup shredded carrots
- 1/4 cup cucumber, sliced
- 1/4 cup red onion, sliced
- 1/2 tablespoon olive oil
- 1/2 tablespoon lemon juice
- 1/4 teaspoon black pepper
- 1/4 teaspoon dried dill

Preparation:
15 Minutes

Servings:
1

Directions:

1. Tuna, mashed avocado, olive oil, lemon juice, black pepper, and dried dill should all be combined in a medium bowl.
2. On a dish, arrange the lettuce leaves.
3. Place the lettuce leaves on top of the tuna mixture.
4. Add red onion, cucumber, and carrot slices on top.
5. To make a wrap, roll the lettuce leaves up.
6. Serve right away.

Macronutrients (per serving): Calories: 249; Carbs: 14g; Protein: 21g; Fat: 14g; Glycemic Index: 20

Shrimp and Broccoli Stir-Fry

Ingredients:

- 8 large raw shrimp, peeled and deveined
- 1 cup broccoli florets
- 1/4 cup sliced red bell pepper
- 1/4 cup sliced yellow onion
- 1 clove garlic, minced
- 1/2 tablespoon olive oil
- 1/2 tablespoon low-sodium soy sauce
- 1/4 teaspoon black pepper
- 1/4 teaspoon ground ginger
- 1/4 teaspoon red pepper flakes

Preparation:
25 Minutes

Servings:
1

Directions:

1. A nonstick skillet should be heated to medium-high.
2. Stir in the olive oil to coat the pan.
3. To the skillet, add the shrimp, broccoli, red bell pepper, and yellow onion. Cook the vegetables and shrimp for a further 2 to 3 minutes, stirring once or twice, until they are both pink. 4. Season the skillet with red pepper flakes, ground ginger, black pepper, and minced garlic. To blend, stir.
4. Low-sodium soy sauce should be drizzled over the stir-fry and mixed in.
5. Serve right away.

Macronutrients (per serving): Calories: 238; Carbs: 14g; Protein: 26g; Fat: 9g; Glycemic Index: 15

Grilled Salmon with Roasted Asparagus

Ingredients:

- 4 oz salmon fillet
- 1/2 tablespoon olive oil
- 1/4 teaspoon black pepper
- 1/4 teaspoon dried dill
- 1/2 lemon, sliced
- 10 spears asparagus
- 1/2 tablespoon balsamic vinegar
- 1/4 teaspoon garlic powder

Preparation:
20 Minutes

Servings:
1

Directions:

1. Set the grill's temperature to medium-high.
2. Combine olive oil, black pepper, and dried dill in a small bowl.
3. Apply the oil mixture to the salmon fillet.
4. Place the salmon skin-side down on the grill and cook for 5-7 minutes.
5. Grill the salmon for an additional 2 to 3 minutes, or until it is thoroughly cooked, after adding the lemon slices.
6. The oven temperature should be set to 400°F (200°C).
7. In a baking dish, toss the asparagus with balsamic vinegar and garlic powder.
8. When tender, roast asparagus for 10 to 12 minutes.
9. Serve grilled salmon with side dishes of roasted asparagus.

Macronutrients (per serving): Calories: 319; Carbs: 12g; Protein: 28g; Fat: 19g; Glycemic Index: 15

Shrimp and Vegetable Skewers

Preparation:
30 Minutes

Servings:
1

Directions:

1. Set the grill's temperature to medium-high.
2. On skewers, arrange the zucchini, red bell pepper, yellow onion, and shrimp.
3. Combine olive oil, balsamic vinegar, black pepper, and dried thyme in a small bowl.
4. Brush the oil mixture on the skewers.
5. Until the shrimp are pink and the vegetables are cooked, grill the skewers for 5 to 7 minutes, flipping once.
6. Serve right away.

Macronutrients (per serving): Calories: 202; Carbs: 14g; Protein: 21g; Fat: 7g; Glycemic Index: 15

Ingredients:

- 8 large raw shrimp, peeled and deveined
- 1/2 red bell pepper, cut into chunks
- 1/2 yellow onion, cut into chunks
- 1/2 zucchini, cut into chunks
- 1/2 tablespoon olive oil
- 1/2 tablespoon balsamic vinegar
- 1/4 teaspoon black pepper
- 1/4 teaspoon dried thyme

Crab-Stuffed Avocado

Ingredients:

- 1/2 avocado, pitted
- 4 oz canned crab meat, drained
- 1/4 cup diced cucumber
- 1/4 cup diced tomato
- 1/4 cup diced red onion
- 1/2 tablespoon olive oil
- 1/2 tablespoon lime juice
- 1/4 teaspoon black pepper
- 1/4 teaspoon dried cilantro

Preparation:
15 Minutes

Servings:
1

Directions:

1. Canned crab meat, diced cucumber, diced tomato, diced red onion, olive oil, lime juice, black pepper, and dried cilantro should all be combined in a medium bowl.
2. Fill the avocado half with the crab mixture.
3. Serve right away.

Macronutrients (per serving): Calories: 252 Carbs: 14g Protein: 15g Fat: 17g; Glycemic Index: 10

Grilled Halibut with Mango Salsa

Ingredients:

- 4 oz halibut fillet
- 1/2 tablespoon olive oil
- 1/4 teaspoon black pepper
- 1/4 teaspoon ground cumin
- 1/2 mango, peeled and diced
- 1/4 cup diced red onion
- 1/4 cup diced red bell pepper
- 1 tablespoon chopped fresh cilantro
- 1/2 tablespoon lime juice

Preparation:
25 Minutes

Servings:
1

Directions:

1. Set the grill's temperature to medium-high.
2. Combine olive oil, ground cumin, and black pepper in a small bowl.
3. The oil mixture should be brushed on the halibut fillet.
4. Halibut should be placed on the grill and cooked through, 5-7 minutes per side.
5. In the meantime, combine lime juice, sliced mango, red onion, red bell pepper, and chopped cilantro in a medium bowl.
6. Halibut should be served grilled with mango salsa on top.

Macronutrients (per serving): Calories: 303; Carbs: 20g; Protein: 29g; Fat: 11g; Glycemic Index: 30

Lemon and Herb Roasted Chicken

Ingredients:

- 4 oz boneless, skinless chicken breast
- 1 tsp olive oil
- 1 garlic clove, minced
- 1 tbsp fresh lemon juice
- 1/4 tsp dried oregano
- 1/4 tsp dried thyme
- 1/2 cup roasted Brussels sprouts
- 1/2 cup roasted sweet potato

Preparation:
50 Minutes

Servings:
1

Directions:

7. Set the oven to 400°F.
8. Olive oil, minced garlic, lemon juice, dried oregano, and dried thyme should be applied to the chicken breast.
9. A baking sheet should be used to roast the chicken breast for 25 to 30 minutes, or until it is thoroughly done.
10. Roast the sweet potato and Brussels sprouts on a different baking sheet in the oven for 20 to 25 minutes, or until they are fork-tender and lightly browned, while the chicken is cooking.
11. Serve roasted chicken with lemon and herbs alongside roasted sweet potato and Brussels sprouts.

Macronutrients (per serving): Calories: 400; Carbs: 34g; Protein: 34g; Fat: 14g; Glycemic Index: 50

Soup and Stew Recipes

Lentil and Vegetable Stew

Preparation:
45 Minutes

Servings:
4

Ingredients:

- 1 tablespoon olive oil
- 1 onion, chopped
- 2 garlic cloves, minced
- 1 teaspoon cumin
- 1 teaspoon coriander
- 1/2 teaspoon turmeric
- 1 cup dry green lentils
- 4 cups vegetable broth
- 2 cups chopped vegetables (carrots, celery, zucchini, etc.)
- 1 can (14.5 ounces) diced tomatoes
- Salt and pepper, to taste

Directions:

1. Olive oil should be heated in a sizable pot over medium heat. About 5 minutes after adding the onion, it should be transparent.
2. Stirring continuously, sauté the garlic, cumin, coriander, and turmeric for one more minute.
3. Lentils, vegetable broth, produce, and tomatoes should all be included. To blend, stir.
4. The stew should be brought to a boil, then simmer for 30 minutes, or until the lentils are soft, on low heat.
5. To taste, add salt and pepper to the food.

Macronutrients (per serving): Calories: 284; Carbs: 45g; Protein: 16g; Fat: 5g; Glycemic Index: 35

Butternut Squash and Apple Soup

Ingredients:

- 1 tablespoon olive oil
- 1 onion, chopped
- 2 garlic cloves, minced
- 1 butternut squash, peeled and diced
- 2 apples, peeled and diced
- 4 cups vegetable broth
- 1/2 teaspoon cinnamon
- 1/4 teaspoon nutmeg
- Salt and pepper, to taste

Preparation:
40 Minutes

Servings:
4

Directions:

1. Olive oil should be heated in a sizable pot over medium heat. About 5 minutes after adding the onion, it should be transparent.
2. Add the apples, applesauce, and garlic. While intermittently stirring, cook for 5 minutes.
3. Add the nutmeg, cinnamon, and vegetable broth. To blend, stir.
4. The soup should be brought to a boil, then simmer for 20 to 25 minutes, or until the veggies are fork-tender, on low heat.
5. Pour the soup into a blender or use an immersion blender to puree it.
6. To taste, add salt and pepper to the food.

Macronutrients (per serving): Calories: 149; Carbs: 30g; Protein: 2g; Fat: 4g; Glycemic Index: 35

Moroccan Chicken Stew

Ingredients:

- 1 tablespoon olive oil
- 1 onion, chopped
- 2 garlic cloves, minced
- 1 teaspoon ground ginger
- 1 teaspoon ground cumin
- 1 teaspoon paprika
- 1/2 teaspoon cinnamon
- 4 chicken thighs, boneless and skinless
- 2 cups chopped vegetables (carrots, bell peppers, zucchini, etc.)
- 1 can (14.5 ounces) diced tomatoes
- 2 cups chicken broth
- 1/2 cup chopped dried apricots
- 1/4 cup chopped fresh parsley
- Salt and pepper, to taste

Preparation:
50 Minutes

Servings:
4

Directions:

1. Olive oil should be heated in a sizable pot over medium heat. About 5 minutes after adding the onion, it should be transparent.
2. Add the cinnamon, paprika, cumin, garlic, and ginger. Stirring continuously, cook for one more minute.
3. Add the chicken thighs, then brown them for five minutes on each side.
4. Add the diced tomatoes, chicken broth, chopped veggies, and dried apricots. To blend, stir.
5. When the chicken is cooked through and the vegetables are soft, turn the heat down to low and let the stew simmer for 30-35 minutes.
6. With a fork, remove the chicken from the pot and shred it. Stir to blend before adding the chicken back to the pot.
7. To taste, add salt and pepper to the food.
8. Before serving, add some chopped parsley as a garnish.

Macronutrients (per serving): Calories: 298; Carbs: 26g; Protein: 29g; Fat: 8g; Glycemic Index: 35

Lemon and Herb Roasted Chicken

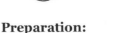

Preparation:
40 Minutes

Servings:
4

Directions:

1. Olive oil is heated over medium heat in a big pot.
2. Garlic and onion should be added and sautéed until transparent.
3. Add the tomatoes, cumin, paprika, chickpeas, and vegetable broth. To blend, stir.
4. Cook for 20 minutes after bringing to a simmer.
5. After adding, simmer the spinach for a further 5 minutes, or until wilted.
6. To taste, add salt and pepper to the food.

Macronutrients (per serving): Calories: 188; Carbs: 27g; Protein: 8g; Fat: 6g; Glycemic Index: 45

Ingredients:

- 2 tbsp olive oil
- 1 onion, diced
- 3 cloves garlic, minced
- 1 can chickpeas, drained and rinsed
- 1 can dice tomatoes
- 4 cups low-sodium vegetable broth
- 2 cups fresh spinach
- 1 tsp cumin
- 1/2 tsp paprika
- Salt and pepper to taste

Turkey and Vegetable Chili

Ingredients:

- 1 tbsp olive oil
- 1 onion, diced
- 1 red bell pepper, diced
- 2 cloves garlic, minced
- 1 lb ground turkey
- 1 can dice tomatoes
- 2 cups low-sodium vegetable broth
- 1 can black beans, drained and rinsed
- 1 can kidney beans, drained and rinsed
- 2 tsp chili powder
- 1 tsp cumin
- Salt and pepper to taste

Preparation:
45 Minutes

Servings:
6

Directions:

1. Olive oil is heated over medium heat in a big pot.
2. Garlic, red bell pepper, and onion should all be added and sautéed until transparent.
3. Cook till browned after adding the ground turkey.
4. Cumin, chili powder, black beans, kidney beans, diced tomatoes, and vegetable broth should all be added. To blend, stir.
5. Cook for 30 minutes after bringing to a simmer.
6. To taste, add salt and pepper to the food.

Macronutrients per serving (1/6 recipe): Calories: 256; Carbs: 26g; Protein: 23g; Fat: 7g; Glycemic Index: 40

Mushroom Barley Soup

Ingredients:

- 2 tbsp olive oil
- 1 onion, diced
- 2 cloves garlic, minced
- 8 oz mushrooms, sliced
- 1 cup pearl barley
- 4 cups low-sodium vegetable broth
- 2 cups water
- 2 carrots, diced
- 2 celery stalks, diced
- 1 tsp dried thyme
- Salt and pepper to taste

Preparation:
1 hour

Servings:
6

Directions:

1. Olive oil is heated over medium heat in a big pot.
2. Garlic and onion should be added and sautéed until transparent.
3. Add the mushrooms and cook them until soft.
4. Carrots, celery, thyme, vegetable broth, and barley should all be included. To blend, stir.
5. Boil for a few minutes, then turn down the heat and simmer for 45 minutes.
6. To taste, add salt and pepper to the food.

Macronutrients (per serving): Calories: 211; Carbs: 38g; Protein: 5g; Fat: 5g; Glycemic Index: 40

Chicken and Vegetable Stew

Ingredients:

- 1 chicken breast, cubed
- 1 cup mixed vegetables (carrots, celery, onion, bell pepper)
- 1 garlic clove, minced
- 1 tablespoon olive oil
- 1 teaspoon dried thyme
- 1 bay leaf
- 1 cup low-sodium chicken broth
- 1/4 teaspoon black pepper
- 1/4 teaspoon paprika
- 1/4 teaspoon cumin
- 1 tablespoon chopped fresh parsley

Preparation:
20 Minutes

Servings:
1

Directions:

1. In a big pot, warm up the olive oil over medium heat.
2. Cook the chicken for 3–4 minutes, or until it is browned.
3. Vegetables should be somewhat softened after an additional 5 minutes of cooking after the addition of the garlic and vegetables.
4. Add the cumin, paprika, thyme, bay leaf, black pepper, and chicken broth. To blend, stir.
5. When the chicken is cooked through and the veggies are tender, bring to a boil, then lower the heat and allow simmer for 20 minutes.
6. Before serving, take out the bay leaf and top with fresh parsley.

Macronutrients (per serving): Calories: 364; Carbohydrates: 22g; Protein: 43g; Fat: 11g; Glycemic Index: 45

Sweet Potato and Black Bean Soup

Ingredients:

- 2 large sweet potatoes, peeled and diced
- 1 can black beans, drained and rinsed
- 1 small onion, chopped
- 2 cloves garlic, minced
- 1 tbsp olive oil
- 1 tsp ground cumin
- 1 tsp ground coriander
- 1 tsp smoked paprika
- 4 cups low-sodium vegetable broth
- 1 tbsp honey or stevia
- Fresh cilantro, chopped, for garnish

Preparation:
30 Minutes

Servings:
4

Directions:

1. Olive oil is heated over medium heat in a big pot. Add the onion and garlic, and cook for about 5 minutes, or until tender.
2. Sweet potatoes, cumin, coriander, and smoked paprika should all be added to the pot. Stirring sporadically, cook for 2-3 minutes.
3. Bring vegetable broth to a boil in the pot after adding the liquid. Sweet potatoes should be cooked for 15 to 20 minutes at low heat with the lid on.
4. Black beans should be added to the stew and simmered for an additional 5 to 10 minutes.
5. The pot should be taken off the heat so it can cool a little. Puree soup until smooth using an immersion blender or by transferring it to a blender.
6. To taste, add stevia or honey.
7. Add fresh cilantro as a garnish after ladling the soup into dishes.

Macronutrients (per serving): Calories: 211; Carbs: 40g; Protein: 7g; Fat: 3g; Glycemic Index: 55

Beef and Vegetable Stew

Preparation:
30 Minutes

Servings:
1

Ingredients:

- 1/2 tablespoon olive oil
- 1/2 pound beef stew meat, cut into small pieces
- 1/4 cup chopped onion
- 1/4 cup chopped celery
- 1/4 cup chopped carrots
- 1/2 cup chopped zucchini
- 1/2 cup chopped mushrooms
- 1/2 cup chopped tomato
- 1/4 teaspoon black pepper
- 1/4 teaspoon garlic powder
- 1/4 teaspoon dried thyme
- 1/4 teaspoon dried rosemary
- 1 1/2 cups beef broth
- 1 tablespoon cornstarch
- 1 tablespoon water

Directions:

1. Olive oil should be heated over medium-high heat in a big pot or Dutch oven.
2. Add the steak and heat it until it is evenly browned.
3. Add the tomato, onion, celery, carrots, zucchini, and mushrooms.
4. Add rosemary, thyme, garlic powder, and black pepper for seasoning.
5. Bring to a boil after adding beef broth.
6. Reduce heat to medium and simmer for 15 to 20 minutes, or until beef is thoroughly cooked and the vegetables are soft.
7. Cornstarch and water should be whipped together in a small basin.
8. Stir the cornstarch mixture into the stew as it thickens.
9. Serve warm.

Macronutrients (per serving): Calories: 375; Carbs: 20g; Protein: 33g; Fat: 18g; Glycemic Index: 50

Turkey and Sweet Potato Stew

Preparation:
35 Minutes

Servings:
1

Ingredients:

- 1/2 tablespoon olive oil
- 1/2 pound ground turkey
- 1/4 cup chopped onion
- 1/4 cup chopped celery
- 1/4 cup chopped carrots
- 1/2 cup chopped sweet potato
- 1/2 cup chopped tomato
- 1/4 teaspoon black pepper
- 1/4 teaspoon garlic powder
- 1/4 teaspoon dried thyme
- 1/4 teaspoon dried sage
- 1 1/2 cups chicken broth
- 1 tablespoon cornstarch
- 1 tablespoon water

Directions:

1. Olive oil should be heated over medium-high heat in a big pot or Dutch oven.
2. Add the ground turkey and heat, breaking it up into little pieces as it cooks, until it is browned.
3. Add the tomato, sweet potato, onion, celery, and carrots.
4. Add thyme, sage, garlic powder, and black pepper to the food to season.
5. Bring to a boil after adding chicken broth.
6. Reduce heat to medium and simmer for 15 to 20 minutes, or until turkey is thoroughly cooked and vegetables are soft.
7. Cornstarch and water should be whipped together in a small basin.
8. Stir the cornstarch mixture into the stew as it thickens.
9. Serve warm.

Macronutrients (per serving): Calories: 320; Carbs: 22g; Protein: 33g; Fat: 11g; Glycemic Index: 40

Salad Recipes

Quinoa and Veggie Salad

Preparation:
20 Minutes

Servings:
1

Directions:

1. Combine the quinoa, finely cut veggies, and fresh herbs in a big bowl.
2. To create the dressing, combine the olive oil, lemon juice, honey (or stevia), black pepper, and garlic powder in a different bowl.
3. Toss the salad with the dressing after pouring it over it.
4. Offer cold.

Macronutrients (per serving): Calories: 310; Carbs: 36g; Protein: 8g; Fat: 15g; Glycemic Index: 15

Ingredients:

- 1/2 cup cooked quinoa
- 1 cup chopped mixed vegetables (e.g. bell peppers, cucumbers, carrots, cherry tomatoes)
- 1/4 cup chopped fresh herbs (e.g. parsley, mint, basil)
- 1 tablespoon olive oil
- 1 tablespoon lemon juice
- 1/2 tablespoon honey or stevia
- 1/4 teaspoon black pepper
- 1/4 teaspoon garlic powder

Spinach and Berry Salad

Ingredients:

- 2 cups baby spinach leaves
- 1/2 cup mixed berries (e.g. strawberries, blueberries, raspberries)
- 1/4 cup chopped walnuts
- 1/4 cup crumbled feta cheese
- 1 tablespoon olive oil
- 1 tablespoon balsamic vinegar
- 1/2 tablespoon honey or stevia
- 1/4 teaspoon black pepper
- 1/4 teaspoon dried basil

Preparation:
15 Minutes

Servings:
1

Directions:

1. Baby spinach leaves, mixed berries, chopped walnuts, and crumbled feta cheese are all combined in a big bowl.
2. The dressing is made by combining olive oil, balsamic vinegar, honey (or stevia), black pepper, and dried basil in a separate bowl.
3. Toss the salad with the dressing after pouring it over it.
4. Offer cold.

Macronutrients (per serving): Calories: 330; Carbs: 20g; Protein: 7g; Fat: 26g; Glycemic Index: 20

Chickpea and Veggie Salad

Ingredients:

- 1/2 cup canned chickpeas, rinsed and drained
- 1 cup chopped mixed vegetables (e.g. bell peppers, cucumbers, cherry tomatoes)
- 1/4 cup chopped fresh herbs (e.g. parsley, cilantro, mint)
- 1 tablespoon olive oil
- 1 tablespoon lemon juice
- 1/2 tablespoon honey or stevia
- 1/4 teaspoon black pepper
- 1/4 teaspoon ground cumin

Preparation:
20 Minutes

Servings:
1

Directions:

1. Chickpeas, chopped veggies, and fresh herbs should all be combined in a big bowl.
2. To create the dressing, combine the olive oil, lemon juice, honey (or stevia), black pepper, and ground cumin in a separate bowl.
3. Toss the salad with the dressing after pouring it over it.
4. Offer cold.

Macronutrients (per serving): Calories: 290; Carbs: 31g; Protein: 8g; Fat: 16g; Glycemic Index: 5

Spinach and Berry Salad

Ingredients:

- 2 cups baby spinach leaves
- 1/2 cup mixed berries (e.g. strawberries, blueberries, raspberries)
- 1/4 cup chopped walnuts
- 1/4 cup crumbled feta cheese
- 1 tablespoon olive oil
- 1 tablespoon balsamic vinegar
- 1/2 tablespoon honey or stevia
- 1/4 teaspoon black pepper
- 1/4 teaspoon dried basil

Preparation:
15 Minutes

Servings:
1

Directions:

1. Baby spinach leaves, mixed berries, chopped walnuts, and crumbled feta cheese are all combined in a big bowl.
2. The dressing is made by combining olive oil, balsamic vinegar, honey (or stevia), black pepper, and dried basil in a separate bowl.
3. Toss the salad with the dressing after pouring it over it.
4. Offer cold.

Macronutrients (per serving): Calories: 330; Carbs: 20g; Protein: 7g; Fat: 26g; Glycemic Index: 10

Apple and Walnut Salad

Ingredients:

- 2 cups mixed greens (e.g. spinach, arugula, lettuce)
- 1 medium apple, thinly sliced
- 1/4 cup chopped walnuts
- 1/4 cup crumbled blue cheese
- 1 tablespoon olive oil
- 1 tablespoon apple cider vinegar
- 1/2 tablespoon honey or stevia
- 1/4 teaspoon black pepper
- 1/4 teaspoon dried thyme

Preparation:
15 Minutes

Servings:
1

Directions:

1. Mix greens, apple pieces, chopped walnuts, and crumbled blue cheese in a big bowl.
2. The dressing is made by combining olive oil, apple cider vinegar, honey (or stevia), black pepper, and dried thyme in a separate bowl.
3. Toss the salad with the dressing after pouring it over it.
4. Offer cold.

Macronutrients (per serving): Calories: 350; Carbs: 24g; Protein: 7g; Fat: 27g; Glycemic Index: 15

Turkey and Sweet Potato Stew

Preparation:
30 Minutes

Servings:
1

Ingredients:

- 1 small chicken breast, grilled and sliced
- 1/2 cup cooked quinoa
- 1 cup mixed greens (e.g. spinach, arugula, lettuce)
- 1/4 cup chopped cucumber
- 1/4 cup chopped cherry tomatoes
- 1/4 cup crumbled feta cheese
- 1 tablespoon olive oil
- 1 tablespoon balsamic vinegar
- 1/2 tablespoon honey or stevia
- 1/4 teaspoon black pepper
- 1/4 teaspoon dried basil

Directions:

1. Grilled chicken, cooked quinoa, mixed greens, diced cucumber, chopped cherry tomatoes, and crumbled feta cheese should all be combined in a big bowl.
2. The dressing is made by combining olive oil, balsamic vinegar, honey (or stevia), black pepper, and dried basil in a separate bowl.
3. Toss the salad with the dressing after pouring it over it.
4. Offer cold.

Macronutrients (per serving): Calories: 480; Carbs: 30g; Protein: 35g; Fat: 23g; Glycemic Index: 15

Spicy Shrimp and Avocado Salad

Ingredients:

- 6 medium shrimp, peeled and deveined
- 1 small avocado, diced
- 1/2 cup cooked quinoa
- 1 cup mixed greens (e.g. spinach, arugula, lettuce)
- 1/4 cup chopped red onion
- 1/4 cup chopped fresh cilantro
- 1 tablespoon olive oil
- 1 tablespoon lime juice
- 1/4 teaspoon cumin
- 1/4 teaspoon chili powder
- 1/4 teaspoon paprika
- Pinch of cayenne pepper

Preparation:
25 Minutes

Servings:
1

Directions:

1. Combine cumin, chili powder, paprika, and cayenne pepper in a small bowl. Toss the shrimp in the mixture to coat.
2. Combine avocado, cooked quinoa, mixed greens, red onion, and fresh cilantro in a different bowl.
3. Make the dressing by combining lime juice and olive oil in a separate bowl.
4. Over medium-high heat, preheat a nonstick pan. When the shrimp are pink and opaque, add them and fry them for two to three minutes on each side.
5. Toss the salad with the cooked shrimp added before topping it with the remaining dressing.
6. Offer cold.

Macronutrients (per serving): Calories: 410; Carbs: 25g; Protein: 20g; Fat: 29g; Glycemic Index: 20

Strawberry, Feta, and Spinach Salad

Ingredients:

- 1 cup baby spinach leaves
- 1/2 cup sliced fresh strawberries
- 1/4 cup crumbled feta cheese
- 1/4 cup chopped walnuts
- 1 tablespoon olive oil
- 1 tablespoon balsamic vinegar
- 1/2 tablespoon honey or stevia
- 1/4 teaspoon black pepper

Preparation:
35 Minutes

Servings:
1

Directions:

1. Baby spinach leaves, fresh strawberry slices, feta cheese crumbles, and chopped walnuts should all be combined in a big bowl.
2. To create the dressing, combine the olive oil, balsamic vinegar, honey (or stevia), and black pepper in a separate bowl.
3. Toss the salad with the dressing after pouring it over it.
4. Offer cold.

Macronutrients (per serving): Calories: 350; Carbs: 15g; Protein: 9g; Fat: 31g; Glycemic Index: 15

Mango and Black Bean Salad

Ingredients:

- 1/2 cup cooked black beans
- 1/2 cup diced mango
- 1/4 cup diced red onion
- 1/4 cup chopped fresh cilantro
- 1/2 jalapeño pepper, seeded and diced
- 1 tablespoon olive oil
- 1 tablespoon lime juice
- 1/4 teaspoon cumin
- Salt and pepper to taste

Preparation:
20 Minutes

Servings:
1

Directions:

1. Cooked black beans, diced mango, red onion, fresh cilantro, and jalapenos peppers should all be combined in a big bowl.
2. To create the dressing, combine the olive oil, cumin, lime juice, salt, and pepper in a separate bowl.
3. Toss the salad with the dressing after pouring it over it.
4. Offer cold.

Macronutrients (per serving): Calories: 290; Carbs: 38g: Protein: 7g: Fat: 13g; Glycemic Index: 20

Pear Salad and Grilled Chicken

Preparation:
30 Minutes

Servings:
1

Ingredients:

- 3 ounces boneless, skinless chicken breast
- 1/2 pear, sliced
- 1 cup mixed greens
- 1/4 cup crumbled blue cheese
- 1/4 cup chopped walnuts
- 1 tablespoon olive oil
- 1 tablespoon apple cider vinegar
- 1 teaspoon honey or stevia
- Salt and pepper to taste

Directions:

1. Grill or grill pan should be heated to medium-high. Salt and pepper the chicken breast before grilling it for 6 to 8 minutes on each side, or until it is thoroughly cooked. After 5 minutes of resting, slice into thin strips.
2. Combine mixed greens, blue cheese crumbles, pear slices, and chopped walnuts in a big bowl.
3. To create the dressing, combine the olive oil, apple cider vinegar, honey or stevia, salt, and pepper in a separate bowl.
4. Toss the salad with the dressing after pouring it over it.
5. Add the grilled chicken strips to the salad as a garnish.
6. Serve right away

Macronutrients (per serving): Calories: 450; Carbs: 19g; Protein: 31g; Fat: 28g; Glycemic Index: 5

Vegetable and Side Recipes

Roasted Brussels Sprouts and Sweet Potatoes

Preparation:
30 Minutes

Servings:
1

Directions:
1. Set the oven to 400°F.
2. Combine the sweet potato, Brussels sprouts, smoked paprika, cinnamon, ginger, honey, or stevia in a big bowl.
3. On a baking sheet, distribute the vegetables in a single layer.
4. Vegetables should be roasted in the oven for 20 to 25 minutes, or until they are soft and browned.
5. As a side dish, serve warm.

Macronutrients (per serving): Calories: 230; Carbs: 36g; Protein: 4g; Fat: 9g; Glycemic Index: 30

Ingredients:

- 1/2 cup Brussels sprouts, trimmed and halved
- 1/2 cup sweet potato, peeled and diced
- 1 tablespoon olive oil
- 1/2 teaspoon smoked paprika
- 1/4 teaspoon cinnamon
- 1/4 teaspoon ground ginger
- 1 tablespoon honey or stevia

Cauliflower Fried Rice

Ingredients:

- 1 cup cauliflower rice
- 1/2 cup diced carrots
- 1/2 cup diced bell peppers
- 1/4 cup chopped scallions
- 1/4 cup frozen peas
- 1 egg, beaten
- 1 tablespoon coconut oil
- 1 tablespoon low-sodium soy sauce or tamari
- 1 teaspoon honey or stevia
- 1/4 teaspoon ground ginger
- Salt and pepper to taste

Preparation:
30 Minutes

Servings:
1

Directions:
1. Warm up the coconut oil in a sizable skillet or wok over medium heat. Cook the sliced carrots for 5 minutes, or until they start to soften.
2. Cook the diced bell peppers for a further 3 to 4 minutes, or until they begin to soften.
3. Frozen peas, cauliflower rice, and chopped onions should all be added to the skillet. Cook the cauliflower rice for 5-7 minutes, or until it is cooked through.
4. Pour the beaten egg into the empty space left by pushing the veggies to the edge of the skillet. The egg should be cooked through before being mixed with the vegetables.
5. To make the sauce, combine low-sodium tamari or soy sauce, honey or stevia, ground ginger, salt, and pepper in a small bowl.
6. Stirring is necessary after adding the sauce to the cauliflower fried rice.
7. Serve warm.

Macronutrients (per serving): Calories: 290; Carbs: 27g; Protein: 11g; Fat: 16g; Glycemic Index: 30

Zucchini Noodles with Avocado Pesto

Ingredients:

- 1 medium zucchini, spiralized or julienned into noodles
- 1/2 avocado, peeled and pitted
- 1/4 cup fresh basil leaves
- 1/4 cup fresh spinach leaves
- 1 tablespoon chopped walnuts
- 1 tablespoon olive oil
- 1 clove garlic, minced
- 1 tablespoon lemon juice
- Salt and pepper to taste

Preparation:
20 Minutes

Servings:
1

Directions:

1. Avocado, basil, spinach, chopped walnuts, olive oil, minced garlic, lemon juice, salt, and pepper can all be combined in a blender or food processor. The avocado pesto is made by blending all the ingredients until smooth.
2. 1 tablespoon of olive oil is heated at medium-high heat in a big skillet. Zucchini noodles should be added and cooked for two to three minutes until crisp and tender.
3. Zucchini noodles and avocado pesto are added to the skillet and combined.
4. Serve warm.

Macronutrients (per serving): Calories: 320; Carbs: 15g; Protein: 6g; Fat: 3g; Glycemic Index: 25

Strawberry, Feta, and Spinach Salad

Ingredients:

- 1 bunch of asparagus, trimmed
- 1 tablespoon olive oil
- 1 tablespoon freshly squeezed lemon juice
- 1 tablespoon grated Parmesan cheese
- 1/4 teaspoon garlic powder
- Salt and pepper to taste

Preparation:
20 Minutes

Servings:
1

Directions:

1. Grill or grill pan should be heated to medium-high.
2. To make the marinade, combine the olive oil, Parmesan cheese, lemon juice, garlic powder, salt, and pepper in a small bowl.
3. Make sure the asparagus spears are evenly coated with the marinade by brushing it on.
4. Grill the asparagus spears for 5 to 7 minutes, or until they are tender and gently browned.
5. Serve warm.

Macronutrients (per serving): Calories: 115; Carbs: 7g; Protein: 7g; Fat: 8g; Glycemic Index: 35

Roasted Carrots with Tahini Yogurt Sauce

Ingredients:

- 1 large carrot, peeled and sliced into thick rounds
- 1 tablespoon olive oil
- 1/4 teaspoon ground cumin
- Salt and pepper to taste

For the Tahini Yogurt Sauce:
- 1 tablespoon tahini
- 1 tablespoon plain Greek yogurt
- 1 tablespoon freshly squeezed lemon juice
- 1/4 teaspoon ground cumin
- Salt and pepper to taste

Preparation:
30 Minutes

Servings:
1

Directions:

1. Set the oven's temperature to 400°F (200°C).
2. Sliced carrots should be coated evenly in a basin with olive oil, cumin, salt, and pepper.
3. On a baking sheet, spread the carrots out in a single layer and roast for 20 to 25 minutes, or until they are soft and gently browned.
4. Make the Tahini Yogurt Sauce while the carrots are roasting. The tahini, Greek yogurt, lemon juice, cumin, salt, and pepper should all be thoroughly combined in a small bowl.
5. Serve the hot roasted carrots with a dab of the tahini yogurt sauce.

Macronutrients (per serving): Calories: 190; Carbs: 11g; Protein: 4g; Fat: 16g; Glycemic Index: 40

Grilled Eggplant with Pesto and Tomatoes

Ingredients:

- 1 small eggplant, sliced into 1/2-inch rounds
- 1 tablespoon olive oil
- Salt and pepper to taste
- 2 tablespoons pesto (homemade or store-bought)
- 1/4 cup diced tomatoes

Preparation:
30 Minutes

Servings:
1

Directions:

1. A grill or grill pan should be preheated to high heat.
2. Slices of eggplant are seasoned with salt and pepper after being brushed with olive oil.
3. The eggplant should be grilled for 3–4 minutes per side or until it is soft and gently browned.
4. Over the grilled eggplant slices, spread the pesto.
5. Serve the hot eggplant with diced tomatoes on top.

Macronutrients (per serving): Calories: 250; Carbs: 16g; Protein: 3g; Fat: 21g; Glycemic Index: 20

Roasted Cauliflower with Curry Yogurt Sauce

Ingredients:

For the roasted cauliflower:
- 1/2 head cauliflower, cut into small florets
- 1 tablespoon olive oil
- Salt and pepper to taste
- 1/4 teaspoon turmeric
- 1/4 teaspoon cumin
- 1/4 teaspoon paprika

For the curry yogurt sauce:
- 1/4 cup plain Greek yogurt
- 1/2 teaspoon curry powder
- 1/2 teaspoon honey
- 1/4 teaspoon grated fresh ginger
- 1/4 teaspoon garlic powder

Preparation:
35 Minutes

Servings:
1

Directions:
1. Set the oven to 400°F.
2. Sprinkle the cauliflower florets with paprika, cumin, turmeric, salt, and olive oil.
3. On a baking sheet, spread the cauliflower out in a single layer.
4. Roast the cauliflower for 25 to 30 minutes, tossing once or twice, or until it is soft and gently browned.
5. Make the curry yogurt sauce by combining yogurt, curry powder, honey, ginger, and garlic powder in a small bowl while the cauliflower roasts.
6. Serve the hot roasted cauliflower with the curry yogurt sauce drizzled over it.

Macronutrients (per serving): Calories: 220; Carbs: 19g; Protein: 10g; Fat: 13g; Glycemic Index: 30

Roasted Vegetable Quinoa Bowl with Avocado Dressing

Preparation:
45 Minutes

Servings:
1

Ingredients:

- 1/2 cup cooked quinoa
- 1/2 small sweet potato, peeled and cubed
- 1/2 cup Brussels sprouts, trimmed and halved
- 1/2 small red onion, sliced
- 1/2 small red bell pepper, seeded and sliced
- 1 tablespoon olive oil
- 1/4 teaspoon smoked paprika
- 1/4 teaspoon garlic powder
- 1/4 teaspoon black pepper
- 1/4 avocado
- 1/2 tablespoon lime juice
- 1/4 teaspoon honey or stevia
- 1 tablespoon water
- 1 tablespoon chopped cilantro
- Optional: 1/4 cup canned black beans, rinsed and drained

Directions:
1. Set the oven to 400°F.
2. Combine the sweet potato, Brussels sprouts, red onion, and red bell pepper with the black pepper, smoky paprika, garlic powder, and olive oil in a mixing bowl.
3. On a baking sheet, arrange the vegetables in a single layer, and roast for 25 to 30 minutes, or until they are soft and lightly browned.
4. Combine the avocado, lime juice, honey or stevia, water, and cilantro in a blender or food processor. Blend till creamy and smooth.
5. Combine the cooked quinoa and roasted vegetables in a serving bowl. Black beans and the avocado dressing go on top (if using).

Macronutrients (per serving): Calories: 440 kcal; Carbs: 60 g; Protein: 11 g; Fat: 19 g; Glycemic Index: 20

Baked Sweet Potato Fries with Avocado Dip

Ingredients:

For the sweet potato fries:
- 1 small sweet potato, peeled and cut into fries
- 1 tablespoon olive oil
- 1/2 teaspoon paprika
- 1/4 teaspoon garlic powder
- 1/4 teaspoon black pepper

For the avocado dip:
- 1/2 ripe avocado, peeled and pitted
- 1 tablespoon plain Greek yogurt
- 1/2 teaspoon lime juice
- 1/4 teaspoon cumin
- 1/4 teaspoon chili powder
- 1/4 teaspoon salt

Preparation: 40 Minutes

Servings: 1

Directions:

1. Set the oven's temperature to 425°F (220°C).
2. Sweet potato fries should be coated equally with olive oil, paprika, garlic powder, and black pepper in a bowl.
3. On a baking sheet covered with parchment paper, arrange the sweet potato fries in a single layer.
4. Bake the sweet potato fries for 25 minutes, or until they are crisp and browned.
5. Make the avocado dip while the sweet potato fries are baking. Smoothly mash the avocado in a small bowl.
6. To the mashed avocado, add the Greek yogurt, lime juice, cumin, chili powder, and salt. Stir to incorporate.
7. Serve the heated sweet potato fries with the accompanying avocado dip.

Macronutrients (per serving): Calories: 378; Carbohydrates: 33g; Protein: 6g; Fat: 27g; Glycemic Index: 40

Stuffed Bell Peppers with Brown Rice and Chickpeas

Ingredients:

- 2 bell peppers, tops removed and seeded
- 1/2 cup cooked brown rice
- 1/2 cup canned chickpeas, drained and rinsed
- 1/4 cup chopped onion
- 1/4 cup chopped celery
- 1/4 cup chopped carrot
- 1/4 cup chopped zucchini
- 1 clove garlic, minced
- 1/4 teaspoon ground cumin
- 1/4 teaspoon paprika
- Salt and pepper to taste
- 1 tablespoon olive oil
- 1/4 cup low-sodium vegetable broth

Preparation: 45 Minutes

Servings: 2

Directions:

1. Set the oven's temperature to 375°F (190°C).
2. Cooked brown rice, canned chickpeas, chopped celery, chopped carrot, diced zucchini, minced garlic, cumin, paprika, salt, and pepper should all be combined in a medium bowl.
3. Place some of the rice and chickpea mixtures inside each bell pepper.
4. Olive oil and low-sodium vegetable broth should be combined in a small basin.
5. Put the filled bell peppers in a baking dish and cover them with the mixture of olive oil and vegetable broth.
6. Bake the peppers in the preheated oven for 30-35 minutes with the foil covering the baking dish, or until they are soft.
7. When the tops are just beginning to lighten in color, remove the foil and bake for a further 5 to 10 minutes.
8. The filled bell peppers should be served hot.

Macronutrients (per serving): Calories: 294; Carbs: 45g; Protein: 10g; Fat: 8g; Glycemic Index: 20

Dessert Recipes

Baked Apples with Cinnamon and Almonds

Preparation:
35 Minutes

Servings:
2

Ingredients:

- 2 medium-sized apples, cored and halved
- 1/4 cup chopped almonds
- 1/2 teaspoon ground cinnamon
- 1 tablespoon honey or stevia
- 1 tablespoon unsalted butter, melted
- 1/4 cup water

Directions:

1. Set the oven's temperature to 375°F (190°C).
2. Almonds that have been chopped, ground cinnamon, and honey or stevia should all be combined in a small basin.
3. Put the cut side of the apple halves in a baking dish.
4. Fill the apple halves' centers with the almond mixture.
5. On top of the apple halves, drizzle the melted unsalted butter.
6. Fill the baking dish's bottom with water.
7. When the apples are soft, bake the baking dish for 20 to 25 minutes in a preheated oven.
8. When the tops are just beginning to lighten in color, remove the foil and bake for a further 5 to 10 minutes.
9. Serve the hot baked apples with any sauce that is still in the baking dish.

Macronutrients (per serving): Calories: 174; Carbs: 26g; Protein: 3g; Fat: 8g; Glycemic Index: 50

Berry Chia Seed Pudding

Ingredients:

- 1 cup unsweetened almond milk
- 1/4 cup chia seeds
- 2 tablespoons honey or stevia
- 1/2 teaspoon vanilla extract
- 1 cup mixed berries (fresh or frozen)
- 1/4 cup chopped walnuts (optional)

Preparation:
10 minutes

Servings:
2

Chilling Time:
4 hour

Directions:

1. Combine the unsweetened almond milk, chia seeds, honey or stevia, and vanilla essence in a medium bowl.
2. The components should be thoroughly mixed after whisking.
3. To keep the chia seeds from clumping, give the mixture a few minutes to settle before whisking it once more.
4. Evenly distribute the chia seed pudding mixture between the two serving bowls.
5. Refrigerate the dishes for at least 4 hours or overnight after wrapping them in plastic wrap.
6. If preferred, sprinkle chopped walnuts and mixed berries on top of the chia seed pudding just before serving.

Macronutrients (per serving): Calories: 228; Carbs: 25g; Protein: 6g; Fat: 13g; Glycemic Index: 45

Chocolate Avocado Pudding

Ingredients:

- 1 ripe avocado, pitted and peeled
- 1/4 cup unsweetened cocoa powder
- 1/4 cup almond milk
- 2 tablespoons honey or stevia
- 1/4 teaspoon vanilla extract
- Pinch of salt

Preparation:
10 Minutes

Servings:
2

Directions:

1. Blend the ripe avocado in a blender or food processor until it is completely smooth.
2. Blender ingredients: Almond milk, honey or stevia, unsweetened cocoa powder, vanilla essence, and a dash of salt.
3. Blend the mixture until it is smooth and all the components are thoroughly incorporated.
4. The chocolate avocado pudding should be divided between two plates.
5. Before serving, place the pudding in the refrigerator to chill for at least 30 minutes.
6. If desired, garnish the chilled pudding with chopped nuts or fruit slices.

Macronutrients (per serving): Calories: 184; Carbs: 21g; Protein: 3g; Fat: 12g; Glycemic Index: 40

Roasted Peach with Greek Yogurt and Honey

Ingredients:

- 2 ripe peaches, pitted and halved
- 1 tablespoon coconut oil
- 1 tablespoon honey or stevia
- 1/2 teaspoon ground cinnamon
- 1/2 cup plain Greek yogurt
- 2 tablespoons chopped almonds or walnuts (optional)

Preparation:
10 Minutes

Servings:
2

Cook Time:
20 minutes

Directions:

1. Set the oven's temperature to 400°F (205°C).
2. Place the cut side of the peach halves in a baking dish.
3. Over the peaches, drizzle the melted coconut oil.
4. Combine the ground cinnamon and honey or stevia in a small bowl.
5. Over the peaches, drizzle the honey or stevia mixture.
6. The peaches should be roasted for 15 to 20 minutes in a warm oven, or until they are soft and slightly caramelized.
7. The roasted peaches should be divided between two serving bowls.
8. Add a dollop of plain Greek yogurt on top of each dish of peaches.
9. If preferred, top with chopped almonds or walnuts.

Macronutrients (per serving): Calories: 171; Carbs: 21g; Protein: 5g; Fat: 9g; Glycemic Index: 50

Peanut Butter Banana Ice Cream

Preparation:
10 Minutes

Servings:
2

Freezing Time:
4 hour

Directions:

1. The frozen banana slices should be processed in a food processor or blender until they resemble ice cream.
2. Vanilla extract, honey or stevia, unsweetened almond milk, natural peanut butter, and the blender.
3. Once everything has been well blended, the mixture should be smooth.
4. Fill a freezer-safe container with the mixture, and then freeze it for at least four hours.
5. Allow the ice cream to soften for a few minutes at room temperature before serving.
6. In two serving bowls, divide the peanut butter banana ice cream.
7. If preferred, top the ice cream with a garnish of chopped peanuts before serving.

Macronutrients (per serving): Calories: 255; Carbs: 30g; Protein: 6g; Fat: 14g; Glycemic Index: 35

Ingredients:

- 2 ripe bananas, sliced and frozen
- 1/4 cup natural peanut butter
- 1/4 cup unsweetened almond milk
- 1 tablespoon honey or stevia
- 1/2 teaspoon vanilla extract

Chocolate Chia Pudding with Berries

Ingredients:

- 1/4 cup chia seeds
- 1 cup unsweetened almond milk
- 1 tablespoon unsweetened cocoa powder
- 1 tablespoon honey or stevia
- 1/2 teaspoon vanilla extract
- 1/2 cup mixed berries, fresh or frozen

Preparation: 10 Minutes   **Servings:** 2   **Chilling Time:** 2 hour

Directions:

1. Chia seeds, unsweetened almond milk, chocolate powder, honey (or stevia), and vanilla extract should all be thoroughly blended in a medium basin.
2. When the pudding has thickened, cover the bowl with plastic wrap and refrigerate in the fridge for at least two hours.
3. Make sure there are no lumps in the pudding by vigorously stirring it just before serving.
4. The chocolate chia pudding should be divided between two serving bowls.
5. Add a large handful of mixed berries on the top of each pudding serve.

Macronutrients (per serving): Calories: 170; Carbs: 20g; Protein: 5g; Fat: 9g; Glycemic Index: 30

Apples with Cinnamon and Walnuts

Ingredients:

- 2 medium-sized apples, cored and halved
- 1 tablespoon honey or stevia
- 1 teaspoon ground cinnamon
- 2 tablespoons chopped walnuts

Preparation: 10 Minutes   **Servings:** 2   **Baking Time:** 30 Minutes

Directions:

1. Set the oven's temperature to 350°F (180°C).
2. On a baking sheet, arrange the apple halves cut side up.
3. Combine the ground cinnamon and honey or stevia in a small bowl.
4. The cut side of the apples should be covered with the cinnamon mixture.
5. Over the apples, scatter the chopped walnuts, lightly pressing them into the cinnamon mixture.
6. For 30 minutes, or until the apples are soft and the walnuts are toasted, bake the apples in the preheated oven.
7. Before serving, let the baked apples cool for a while.

Macronutrients (per serving): Calories: 140; Carbs: 23g; Protein: 1g; Fat: 6g; Glycemic Index: 35

Coconut Mango Rice Pudding

Ingredients:

- 1 cup uncooked brown rice
- 2 cups unsweetened coconut milk
- 1/2 cup water
- 1/4 cup honey or stevia
- 1/2 teaspoon ground cardamom
- 1/2 teaspoon ground ginger
- 1/4 teaspoon salt
- 1 ripe mango, peeled and diced
- 2 tablespoons shredded coconut, toasted

Preparation:
10 Minutes

Servings:
2

Cooking Time:
25 Minutes

Chilling Time:
45 Minutes

Directions:

1. Brown rice, unsweetened coconut milk, water, honey, stevia, salt, ground cardamom, and ground ginger should all be combined in a big pot. Over high heat, bring the mixture to a boil.
2. Simmer for 20 to 25 minutes, or until the rice is soft and the liquid has been absorbed, on low heat with the lid on the pan.
3. Mango dice are added to the rice pudding after it has been taken off the heat.
4. Give the rice pudding five to ten minutes to cool.
5. Distribute the rice pudding among the four serving bowls.
6. Refrigerate the rice pudding for at least two hours, or until it is set.
7. Top each dish with the toasted shredded coconut just before serving.

Macronutrients (per serving): Calories: 280; Carbs: 52g; Protein: 4g; Fat: 7g; Glycemic Index: 40

Chocolate Avocado Mousse

Preparation:
10 Minutes

Servings:
2

Chilling Time:
10 Minutes

Directions:

1. Remove the pit from the avocados, cut them in half, and scoop the flesh into a food processor.
2. The unsweetened almond milk, vanilla extract, salt, honey or stevia, unsweetened cocoa powder, and food processor are all added.
3. The mixture should be processed until it is creamy and smooth, scraping down the bowl's sides as necessary.
4. Distribute the chocolate avocado mousse across the four plates.
5. Refrigerate the chocolate avocado mousse for at least an hour, or until it is set.
6. Add fresh berries to the top of each plate before serving.

Macronutrients (per serving): Calories: 210; Carbs: 22g; Protein: 3g; Fat: 15g; Glycemic Index: 45

Ingredients:

- 2 ripe avocados
- 1/4 cup unsweetened cocoa powder
- 1/4 cup honey or stevia
- 1/4 cup unsweetened almond milk
- 1 teaspoon vanilla extract
- Pinch of salt
- Fresh berries, for serving

Blueberry Chia Pudding

Ingredients:

- 1 cup unsweetened almond milk
- 1/4 cup chia seeds
- 2 tablespoons honey or stevia
- 1/2 teaspoon vanilla extract
- 1/2 cup fresh blueberries
- 2 tablespoons chopped walnuts

Preparation:
10 Minutes

Servings:
2

Chilling Time:
10 Minutes

Directions:

1. Mix the unsweetened almond milk, chia seeds, honey or stevia, and vanilla essence in a medium bowl.
2. Gently whisk the blueberries into the mixture after adding them.
3. Evenly distribute the mixture between two tiny bowls or jars.
4. Refrigerate for at least 2 hours, or until the mixture has thickened and set, covering the jars or bowls with plastic wrap.
5. Add chopped walnuts to the top of each jar or bowl before serving.

Macronutrients (per serving): Calories: 210; Carbs: 20g; Protein: 6g; Fat: 12g; Glycemic Index: 40

Juice and Smoothies Recipes

Apple and Walnut Salad

Preparation:
5 Minutes

Servings:
1

Directions:

1. Blend the items together in a blender.
2. Blend till smooth and creamy at high speed.
3. If the mixture is too thick, add a little more almond milk or water to thin it up to the appropriate consistency.
4. Pour into a glass, then sip right away.

Macronutrients (per serving): Calories: 350; Carbs: 40g; Protein: 8g; Fat: 21g; Glycemic Index: 25

Ingredients:

- 1 cup unsweetened almond milk
- 1/2 cup chopped kale
- 1/2 cup chopped spinach
- 1/2 ripe avocado
- 1 small banana, frozen
- 1 tablespoon chia seeds
- 1/2 teaspoon grated fresh ginger
- 1 teaspoon honey or stevia
- 1/2 teaspoon ground cinnamon

Carrot Turmeric Juice

Ingredients:

- 2 medium carrots, washed and peeled
- 1 small apple, cored and quartered
- 1/2 inch piece of fresh ginger, peeled
- 1/2 inch piece of fresh turmeric, peeled
- 1/4 teaspoon ground cinnamon
- 1/4 teaspoon ground cardamom
- 1/2 cup cold water

Preparation:
10 Minutes

Servings:
1

Directions:

1. Slice the ginger, turmeric, apple, and carrots finely.
2. Blend the chopped ingredients with the cinnamon, cardamom, and cool water.
3. The mixture should be smooth and creamy after a minute or two of high-speed blending.
4. Fill a glass with the juice after straining it through a fine-mesh sieve or nut milk bag.
5. Serve right away or keep in the fridge for up to 24 hours.

Macronutrients (per serving): Calories: 150; Carbs: 35g; Protein: 2g; Fat: 1g; Glycemic Index: 20

Apple and Walnut Salad

Ingredients:

- 1 cup unsweetened almond milk
- 1/2 cup frozen mixed berries (blueberries, raspberries, and strawberries)
- 1/2 frozen banana
- 1 tablespoon ground flaxseed
- 1/2 teaspoon vanilla extract
- 1 teaspoon honey or stevia

Preparation:
5 Minutes

Servings:
1

Directions:

1. Blend the items together in a blender.
2. For one to two minutes, or until the mixture is smooth and creamy, blend at high speed.
3. If the mixture is too thick, add a little more almond milk or water to thin it up to the appropriate consistency.
4. Pour into a glass, then sip right away.

Macronutrients (per serving): Calories: 250; Carbs: 38g; Protein: 5g; Fat: 9g; Glycemic Index: 15

Green Detox Smoothie

Ingredients:

- 1/2 cup baby spinach
- 1/2 cup kale leaves
- 1/2 small avocado, pitted and peeled
- 1 small apple, cored and chopped
- 1/2 cup unsweetened almond milk
- 1/2 cup cold water
- 1 tablespoon chia seeds
- 1 tablespoon honey or stevia

Preparation:
10 Minutes

Servings:
1

Directions:

1. Blend the spinach, kale, apple, avocado, water, chia seeds, honey, or stevia in a blender with the almond milk.
2. For one to two minutes, or until the mixture is smooth and creamy, blend at high speed.
3. Add a little water at a time until the proper consistency is achieved if the mixture is too thick.
4. Pour into a glass, then sip right away.

Macronutrients (per serving): Calories: 250; Carbs: 30g; Protein: 5g; Fat: 15g; Glycemic Index: 10

Apple and Walnut Salad

Ingredients:

- 1 medium-sized apple, cored and chopped
- 1 small cucumber, chopped
- 1/2 lemon, juiced
- 1/2 inch piece of fresh ginger, peeled and chopped
- 1/2 inch piece of fresh turmeric, peeled and chopped
- 1/2 cup water
- 1 tablespoon honey or stevia

Preparation:
10 Minutes

Servings:
1

Directions:

1. In a blender, combine the apple, cucumber, ginger, turmeric, water, and honey or stevia.
2. For one to two minutes on high speed, or until the mixture is well blended and smooth.
3. Through a fine-mesh strainer, pour the mixture into a glass.
4. Stir well, then serve right away.

Macronutrients (per serving): Calories: 100; Carbs: 25g; Protein: 1g; Fat: 0g; Glycemic Index: 15

Mango Lassi Smoothie

Ingredients:

- 1 cup chopped ripe mango
- 1/2 cup plain low-fat yogurt
- 1/2 cup unsweetened almond milk
- 1/4 teaspoon ground cardamom
- 1 tablespoon honey or stevia
- 1/4 cup ice cubes

Preparation:
5 Minutes

Servings:
1

Directions:

1. Mango chunks, yogurt, almond milk, cardamom, honey or stevia, and ice cubes should all be combined in a blender.
2. For one to two minutes, or until the mixture is well blended and smooth, blend at high speed.
3. Serve the mixture immediately after pouring it into a glass.

Macronutrients (per serving): Calories: 200; Carbs: 40g;
Protein: 7g; Fat: 3g; Glycemic Index: 25

Beetroot, Carrot, and Ginger Juice

Ingredients:

- 1 medium-sized beetroot, chopped
- 2 medium-sized carrots, chopped
- 1 small piece of ginger, peeled and grated
- 1/2 lemon, juiced
- 1/2 cup water

Preparation:
10 Minutes

Servings:
1

Directions:

1. To a juicer, add the grated ginger, grated carrots, and diced beets.
2. Together with the ginger, juice the vegetables.
3. Mix thoroughly after adding water and lemon juice to the juice.
4. Serve the juice right away by pouring it into a glass.

Macronutrients (per serving): Calories: 110; Carbs: 26g;
Protein: 3g; Fat: 1g; Glycemic Index: 15

Blueberry Almond Butter Smoothie

Ingredients:

- 1 cup frozen blueberries
- 1 banana, sliced and frozen
- 1 tbsp almond butter
- 1/2 cup unsweetened almond milk
- 1 tsp honey or stevia (optional)

Preparation:
5 Minutes

Servings:
1

Directions:

1. Blend the almond milk, almond butter, frozen banana slices, and frozen blueberries in a blender.
2. Blend the ingredients up until they're creamy and smooth.
3. If more sweetness is wanted, add honey or stevia after tasting the smoothie.
4. Serve the smoothie right after pouring it into a glass.

Macronutrients (per serving): Calories: 315; Carbs: 50g; Protein: 7g; Fat: 12g; Glycemic Index: 20

Pineapple Basil Juice

Ingredients:

- 1 cup fresh pineapple chunks
- 5-6 fresh basil leaves
- 1/2 lime, juiced
- 1/2 cup water

Preparation:
10 Minutes

Servings:
1

Directions:

1. To a juicer, add the pineapple pieces and basil leaves.
2. The components are juiced.
3. Juice should be added to a glass.
4. Pour water into the glass after adding the lime juice.
5. To blend, thoroughly stir the juice.
6. If desired, serve the juice over ice right away.

Macronutrients (per serving): Calories: 70; Carbs: 18g; Protein: 1g; Fat: 0.5g; Glycemic Index: 25

Apple and Walnut Salad

Preparation:
10 Minutes

Servings:
1

Directions:

1. Mango, avocado, baby spinach, almond milk, grated ginger, and honey should all be added to a blender.
2. Blend until creamy and smooth on high.
3. Put a glass with the smoothie in it.
4. Serve right away.

Macronutrients (per serving): Calories: 290 Carbs: 40g Protein: 5g Fat: 13g; Glycemic Index: 25

Ingredients:

- 1 ripe mango, peeled and chopped
- 1/2 ripe avocado, peeled and pitted
- 1 cup packed fresh baby spinach
- 1/2 cup unsweetened almond milk
- 1/2 tsp grated fresh ginger
- 1 tsp honey

147-Day Meal Plan

Week 1

Day	Breakfast	Lunch	Snack	Dinner
1	Sweet Potato Breakfast Bowl	Brown Rice and Bean Burrito Bowl	One and a half ounces of dried apricots	Lemon and Herb Roasted Chicken
2	Veggie and Cheese Omelette	Herb-Roasted Chicken Thighs	Reduced-fat whole grain cookie	Grilled Flank Steak with Chimichurri Sauce
3	Banana and Peanut Butter Smoothie	Butternut Squash and Apple Soup	One and a half ounces of dried apricots	Quinoa and Vegetable Stir-Fry
4	Vegetable Frittata	Lentil and Vegetable Stir Fry	One low-sugar cereal bar	Zucchini Noodles with Avocado Pesto
5	Veggie Omelet	Roasted Vegetable Quinoa Bowl with Avocado Dressing	Reduced-fat whole grain cookie	Lentil and Vegetable Stir Fry
6	Overnight Oats with Chia Seeds and Berries	Spicy Chickpea and Spinach Curry	One banana	Grilled Salmon with Roasted Asparagus
7	Vegetable Frittata	Quinoa and Veggie Salad	One pear	Baked Sweet Potato Fries with Avocado Dip

Week 2

Day	Breakfast	Lunch	Snack	Dinner
1	Sweet Potato Breakfast Bowl	Chickpea and Vegetable Stew	One small banana	Roasted Vegetable Quinoa Bowl with Avocado Dressing
2	Avocado Toast with Turkey Bacon	Lentil and Vegetable Stir Fry	One small banana	Broccoli and Mushroom Stir-Fry
3	Berry and Greek Yogurt Parfait	Grilled Asparagus with Lemon and Parmesan	One and a half ounces of dried apricots	Quinoa and Vegetable Salad
4	Avocado Toast with Turkey Bacon	Stuffed Bell Peppers with Brown Rice and Chickpeas	Seven ounces of skim milk	Herb-Roasted Chicken Thighs
5	Vegetable Frittata	Chickpea and Spinach Curry	One pear	Butternut Squash and Apple Soup
6	Whole Grain Porridge	Herb-Roasted Chicken Thighs	One banana	Butternut Squash and Apple Soup
7	Veggie and Cheese Omelette	Brown Rice and Bean Burrito Bowl	One small banana	Grilled Flank Steak with Chimichurri Sauce

Week 3

Day	Breakfast	Lunch	Snack	Dinner
1	Veggie Omelet	Chicken and Vegetable Stew	One rye cracker spread with low-fat soft chees	Cauliflower Rice and Black Bean Bowl
2	Avocado Toast with Egg	Lentil and Vegetable Stir Fry	One rye cracker spread with low-fat soft chees	Turkey and Sweet Potato Stew
3	Veggie Omelet	Lemon and Herb Roasted Chicken	One small banana	Broccoli and Mushroom Stir-Fry
4	Veggie and Cheese Omelette	Lentil and Vegetable Stir Fry	One orange	Butternut Squash and Apple Soup
5	Overnight Oats with Chia Seeds and Berries	Chicken and Vegetable Stew	One banana	Pear Salad and Grilled Chicken
6	Berry and Greek Yogurt Parfait	Zucchini Noodles with Avocado Pesto	One small banana	Pork Chops with Apple Chutney
7	Overnight Oats with Chia Seeds and Berries	Pork Chops with Apple Chutney	One apple	Grilled Salmon with Roasted Asparagus

Week 4

Day	Breakfast	Lunch	Snack	Dinner
1	Berry and Greek Yogurt Parfait	Roasted Carrots with Tahini Yogurt Sauce	Seven ounces of skim milk	Lentil and Vegetable Stir Fry
2	Berry and Greek Yogurt Parfait	Brown Rice and Bean Burrito Bowl	One pear	Herb-Roasted Chicken Thighs
3	Veggie and Cheese Omelette	Lentil and Vegetable Curry	One apple	Pear Salad and Grilled Chicken
4	Avocado Toast with Egg	Quinoa and Vegetable Stir-Fry	One banana	Chickpea and Spinach Soup
5	Veggie Omelet	Roasted Carrots with Tahini Yogurt Sauce	Two sticks of celery filled with low-fat soft chees	Grilled Salmon with Roasted Asparagus
6	Berry and Greek Yogurt Parfait	Roasted Carrots with Tahini Yogurt Sauce	Two sticks of celery filled with low-fat sof	Chickpea and Spinach Curry
7	Veggie and Cheese Omelette	Tuna Avocado Lettuce Wraps	Reduced-fat whole grain cookie	Roasted Cauliflower with Curry Yogurt Sauce

Week 5

Day	Breakfast	Lunch	Snack	Dinner
1	Sweet Potato Breakfast Bowl	Quinoa and Vegetable Stir-Fry	One orange	Tuna Avocado Lettuce Wraps
2	Banana and Peanut Butter Smoothie	Butternut Squash and Apple Soup	One apple	Chickpea and Spinach Curry
3	Veggie Omelet	Mango and Black Bean Salad	One banana	Baked Sweet Potato Fries with Avocado Dip
4	Overnight Oats with Chia Seeds and Berries	Roasted Brussels Sprouts and Sweet Potatoes	One rye cracker spread with low-fat soft chees	Beef and Vegetable Stew
5	Veggie and Cheese Omelette	Herb-Roasted Chicken Thighs	Seven ounces of skim milk	Chickpea and Vegetable Stew
6	Avocado Toast with Egg	Cauliflower Fried Rice	One orange	Pear Salad and Grilled Chicken
7	Veggie and Cheese Omelette	Turkey and Black Bean Chili	One banana	Roasted Brussels Sprouts and Sweet Potatoes

Week 6

Day	Breakfast	Lunch	Snack	Dinner
1	Avocado Toast with Egg	Lentil and Spinach Soup	Two sticks of celery filled with low-fat sof	Pan-Seared Scallops with Roasted Vegetables
2	Avocado Toast with Turkey Bacon	Spicy Shrimp and Avocado Salad	Reduced-fat whole grain cookie	Quinoa and Veggie Salad
3	Avocado Toast with Egg	Grilled Eggplant with Pesto and Tomatoes	One low-sugar cereal bar	Lentil and Vegetable Curry
4	Avocado Toast with Turkey Bacon	Grilled Eggplant with Pesto and Tomatoes	One pear	Baked Sweet Potato Fries with Avocado Dip
5	Whole Grain Porridge	Baked Lemon Salmon with Asparagus	One apple	Sweet Potato and Black Bean Soup
6	Overnight Oats with Chia Seeds and Berries	Garlic and Herb Shrimp Skewers	Two sticks of celery filled with low-fat sof	Baked Salmon with Roasted Vegetables
7	Avocado Toast with Egg	Beef and Vegetable Stew	One orange	Turkey and Vegetable Stir-Fry

Week 7

Day	Breakfast	Lunch	Snack	Dinner
1	Whole Grain Porridge	Cauliflower Fried Rice	Low-fat fruit yogurt	Chicken and Vegetable Stew
2	Berry and Greek Yogurt Parfait	Strawberry, Feta, and Spinach Salad	One and a half ounces of dried apricots	Pork Chops with Apple Chutney
3	Vegetable Frittata	Apple and Walnut Salad	One apple	Beef Stir-Fry
4	Vegetable Frittata	Moroccan Chicken Stew	One apple	Quinoa and Black Bean Salad
5	Avocado Toast with Egg	Grilled Eggplant with Pesto and Tomatoes	One rye cracker spread with low-fat soft chees	Strawberry, Feta, and Spinach Salad
6	Sweet Potato Breakfast Bowl	Stuffed Bell Peppers with Brown Rice and Chickpeas	One banana	Moroccan Chicken Stew
7	Avocado Toast with Egg	Broccoli and Mushroom Stir-Fry	One pear	Quinoa and Vegetable Stir-Fry

Week 8

Day	Breakfast	Lunch	Snack	Dinner
1	Veggie Omelet	Grilled Pork Tenderloin with Peach Salsa	One and a half ounces of dried apricots	Baked Sweet Potato Fries with Avocado Dip
2	Sweet Potato Breakfast Bowl	Zucchini Noodles with Avocado Pesto	Low-fat fruit yogurt	Lentil and Vegetable Stew
3	Veggie Omelet	Quinoa and Vegetable Stir-Fry	One banana	Beef Stir-Fry
4	Vegetable Frittata	Pear Salad and Grilled Chicken	Two sticks of celery filled with low-fat sof	Crab-Stuffed Avocado
5	Veggie and Cheese Omelette	Beef Stir-Fry	Low-fat fruit yogurt	Beef and Vegetable Stew
6	Veggie Omelet	Beef Stir-Fry	Seven ounces of skim milk	Grilled Halibut with Mango Salsa
7	Berry and Greek Yogurt Parfait	Crab-Stuffed Avocado	Seven ounces of skim milk	Brown Rice and Vegetable Stir-Fry

Week 9

Day	Breakfast	Lunch	Snack	Dinner
1	Whole Grain Porridge	Lentil and Vegetable Curry	Reduced-fat whole grain cookie	Cauliflower Fried Rice
2	Veggie and Cheese Omelette	Zucchini and Red Pepper Frittata	Two sticks of celery filled with low-fat soft chees	Broccoli and Mushroom Stir-Fry
3	Avocado Toast with Turkey Bacon	Lentil and Vegetable Stew	One small banana	Grilled Salmon with Roasted Asparagus
4	Vegetable Frittata	Brown Rice and Vegetable Stir-Fry	One orange	Pear Salad and Grilled Chicken
5	Overnight Oats with Chia Seeds and Berries	Roasted Carrots with Tahini Yogurt Sauce	Two sticks of celery filled with low-fat soft chees	Mushroom Barley Soup
6	Banana and Peanut Butter Smoothie	Chickpea and Vegetable Stew	Low-fat fruit yogurt	Brown Rice and Bean Burrito Bowl
7	Banana and Peanut Butter Smoothie	Beef and Vegetable Stew	Seven ounces of skim milk	Turkey and Sweet Potato Stew

Week 10

Day	Breakfast	Lunch	Snack	Dinner
1	Veggie and Cheese Omelette	Grilled Salmon with Roasted Asparagus	Low-fat fruit yogurt	Lentil and Vegetable Curry
2	Whole Grain Porridge	Grilled Halibut with Mango Salsa	One and a half ounces of dried apricots	Spinach and Tofu Stir-Fry
3	Vegetable Frittata	Baked Salmon with Roasted Vegetables	One pear	Grilled Asparagus with Lemon and Parmesan
4	Veggie Omelet	Butternut Squash and Apple Soup	One rye cracker spread with low-fat soft chees	Roasted Vegetable Quinoa Bowl with Avocado Dressing
5	Vegetable Frittata	Baked Lemon Salmon with Asparagus	One apple	Quinoa and Vegetable Salad
6	Veggie and Cheese Omelette	Turkey and Black Bean Chili	One apple	Moroccan Chicken Stew
7	Berry and Greek Yogurt Parfait	Chickpea and Sweet Potato Curry	One small banana	Beef and Vegetable Stew

Week 11

Day	Breakfast	Lunch	Snack	Dinner
1	Veggie and Cheese Omelette	Chickpea and Sweet Potato Curry	Reduced-fat whole grain cookie	Cauliflower Fried Rice
2	Berry and Greek Yogurt Parfait	Spinach and Berry Salad	Two sticks of celery filled with low-fat sof	Strawberry, Feta, and Spinach Salad
3	Banana and Peanut Butter Smoothie	Mushroom Barley Soup	One banana	Grilled Pork Tenderloin with Peach Salsa
4	Overnight Oats with Chia Seeds and Berries	Moroccan Chicken Stew	One and a half ounces of dried apricots	Pear Salad and Grilled Chicken
5	Sweet Potato Breakfast Bowl	Baked Sweet Potato Fries with Avocado Dip	Two sticks of celery filled with low-fat sof	Cauliflower Fried Rice
6	Berry and Greek Yogurt Parfait	Lentil and Spinach Soup	Two sticks of celery filled with low-fat sof	Lentil and Vegetable Stew
7	Avocado Toast with Turkey Bacon	Grilled Chicken and Quinoa Salad	One orange	Turkey and Vegetable Chili

Week 12

Day	Breakfast	Lunch	Snack	Dinner
1	Overnight Oats with Chia Seeds and Berries	Pan-Seared Scallops with Roasted Vegetables	Two sticks of celery filled with low-fat soft chees	Quinoa and Veggie Salad
2	Veggie Omelet	Turkey and Black Bean Chili	One low-sugar cereal bar	Broccoli and Mushroom Stir-Fry
3	Berry and Greek Yogurt Parfait	Grilled Chicken and Quinoa Salad	One and a half ounces of dried apricots	Turkey and Vegetable Stir-Fry
4	Vegetable Frittata	Turkey and Black Bean Chili	One low-sugar cereal bar	Pan-Seared Scallops with Roasted Vegetables
5	Overnight Oats with Chia Seeds and Berries	Brown Rice and Bean Burrito Bowl	One pear	Turkey and Black Bean Chili
6	Whole Grain Porridge	Moroccan Chicken Stew	One small banana	Shrimp and Vegetable Skewers
7	Berry and Greek Yogurt Parfait	Brown Rice and Bean Burrito Bowl	Seven ounces of skim milk	Baked Salmon with Roasted Vegetables

Week 13

Day	Breakfast	Lunch	Snack	Dinner
1	Overnight Oats with Chia Seeds and Berries	Quinoa and Black Bean Salad	One low-sugar cereal bar	Grilled Salmon with Roasted Asparagus
2	Avocado Toast with Turkey Bacon	Turkey and Sweet Potato Stew	Two sticks of celery filled with low-fat soft chees	Grilled Halibut with Mango Salsa
3	Avocado Toast with Turkey Bacon	Pan-Seared Scallops with Roasted Vegetables	One apple	Baked Sweet Potato Fries with Avocado Dip
4	Avocado Toast with Turkey Bacon	Stuffed Bell Peppers with Brown Rice and Chickpeas	One banana	Lentil and Vegetable Curry
5	Veggie and Cheese Omelette	Roasted Cauliflower with Curry Yogurt Sauce	Seven ounces of skim milk	Pan-Seared Scallops with Roasted Vegetables
6	Overnight Oats with Chia Seeds and Berries	Strawberry, Feta, and Spinach Salad	One and a half ounces of dried apricots	Turkey and Vegetable Stir-Fry
7	Berry and Greek Yogurt Parfait	Spicy Shrimp and Avocado Salad	One rye cracker spread with low-fat soft chees	Lemon and Herb Roasted Chicken

Week 14

Day	Breakfast	Lunch	Snack	Dinner
1	Vegetable Frittata	Chicken and Vegetable Stew	One pear	Quinoa Salad with Chickpeas and Vegetables
2	Avocado Toast with Turkey Bacon	Grilled Chicken and Quinoa Salad	One small banana	Zucchini Noodles with Avocado Pesto
3	Overnight Oats with Chia Seeds and Berries	Turkey and Black Bean Chili	Low-fat fruit yogurt	Mango and Black Bean Salad
4	Avocado Toast with Turkey Bacon	Cauliflower Rice and Black Bean Bowl	One small banana	Chickpea and Spinach Soup
5	Veggie and Cheese Omelette	Grilled Tuna Salad	One pear	Roasted Pork Loin with Apple and Onion
6	Whole Grain Porridge	Shrimp and Vegetable Skewers	One small banana	Lentil and Vegetable Stir Fry
7	Vegetable Frittata	Grilled Eggplant with Pesto and Tomatoes	Low-fat fruit yogurt	Apple and Walnut Salad

Week 15

Day	Breakfast	Lunch	Snack	Dinner
1	Veggie Omelet	Cauliflower Fried Rice	Two sticks of celery filled with low-fat soft chees	Lentil and Vegetable Curry
2	Veggie and Cheese Omelette	Baked Sweet Potato Fries with Avocado Dip	One apple	Tuna Avocado Lettuce Wraps
3	Berry and Greek Yogurt Parfait	Mango and Black Bean Salad	One rye cracker spread with low-fat soft chees	Quinoa and Veggie Salad
4	Banana and Peanut Butter Smoothie	Grilled Eggplant with Pesto and Tomatoes	One banana	Lemon and Herb Roasted Chicken
5	Berry and Greek Yogurt Parfait	Quinoa and Black Bean Salad	One pear	Roasted Pork Loin with Apple and Onion
6	Vegetable Frittata	Tuna Avocado Lettuce Wraps	Two sticks of celery filled with low-fat sof	Grilled Flank Steak with Chimichurri Sauce
7	Whole Grain Porridge	Shrimp and Broccoli Stir-Fry	One banana	Grilled Tuna Salad

Week 16

Day	Breakfast	Lunch	Snack	Dinner
1	Avocado Toast with Turkey Bacon	Lentil Soup with Vegetables	One pear	Roasted Vegetable Quinoa Bowl with Avocado Dressing
2	Banana and Peanut Butter Smoothie	Grilled Halibut with Mango Salsa	One banana	Lemon and Herb Roasted Chicken
3	Veggie Omelet	Garlic and Herb Shrimp Skewers	Two sticks of celery filled with low-fat sof	Black Bean and Vegetable Soup
4	Whole Grain Porridge	Lentil and Vegetable Stew	One orange	Cauliflower Rice and Black Bean Bowl
5	Berry and Greek Yogurt Parfait	Pear Salad and Grilled Chicken	One pear	Spicy Chickpea and Spinach Curry
6	Vegetable Frittata	Chickpea and Sweet Potato Curry	Reduced-fat whole grain cookie	Grilled Halibut with Mango Salsa
7	Veggie Omelet	Broccoli and Mushroom Stir-Fry	One apple	Zucchini and Red Pepper Frittata

Week 17

Day	Breakfast	Lunch	Snack	Dinner
1	Vegetable Frittata	Black Bean and Vegetable Soup	One low-sugar cereal bar	Brown Rice and Vegetable Stir-Fry
2	Berry and Greek Yogurt Parfait	Quinoa Salad with Chickpeas and Vegetables	One small banana	Brown Rice and Bean Burrito Bowl
3	Whole Grain Porridge	Roasted Vegetable Quinoa Bowl with Avocado Dressing	One rye cracker spread with low-fat soft chees	Quinoa and Vegetable Salad
4	Overnight Oats with Chia Seeds and Berries	Turkey and Vegetable Stir-Fry	One small banana	Shrimp and Broccoli Stir-Fry
5	Sweet Potato Breakfast Bowl	Zucchini Noodles with Avocado Pesto	Two sticks of celery filled with low-fat sof	Chickpea and Sweet Potato Curry
6	Banana and Peanut Butter Smoothie	Lemon and Herb Roasted Chicken	Reduced-fat whole grain cookie	Baked Salmon with Roasted Vegetables
7	Berry and Greek Yogurt Parfait	Baked Salmon with Roasted Vegetables	One orange	Spicy Shrimp and Avocado Salad

Week 18

Day	Breakfast	Lunch	Snack	Dinner
1	Veggie and Cheese Omelette	Brown Rice and Vegetable Stir-Fry	Reduced-fat whole grain cookie	Brown Rice and Vegetable Stir-Fry
2	Avocado Toast with Turkey Bacon	Grilled Pork Tenderloin with Peach Salsa	One low-sugar cereal bar	Spinach and Berry Salad
3	Avocado Toast with Egg	Broccoli and Mushroom Stir-Fry	One banana	Brown Rice and Vegetable Stir-Fry
4	Vegetable Frittata	Pan-Seared Scallops with Roasted Vegetables	One rye cracker spread with low-fat soft chees	Shrimp and Broccoli Stir-Fry
5	Veggie Omelet	Spinach and Berry Salad	One orange	Beef and Vegetable Stew
6	Avocado Toast with Egg	Grilled Tuna Salad	Reduced-fat whole grain cookie	Lentil and Vegetable Stew
7	Sweet Potato Breakfast Bowl	Mango and Black Bean Salad	One small banana	Grilled Flank Steak with Chimichurri Sauce

Week 19

Day	Breakfast	Lunch	Snack	Dinner
1	Whole Grain Porridge	Pan-Seared Scallops with Roasted Vegetables	One low-sugar cereal bar	Roasted Carrots with Tahini Yogurt Sauce
2	Veggie and Cheese Omelette	Turkey and Vegetable Chili	One orange	Spinach and Berry Salad
3	Veggie and Cheese Omelette	Quinoa and Vegetable Stir-Fry	One and a half ounces of dried apricots	Cauliflower Fried Rice
4	Banana and Peanut Butter Smoothie	Lemon and Herb Roasted Chicken	One low-sugar cereal bar	Grilled Tuna Salad
5	Veggie and Cheese Omelette	Herb-Roasted Chicken Thighs	One small banana	Roasted Cauliflower with Curry Yogurt Sauce
6	Avocado Toast with Egg	Quinoa and Black Bean Salad	Reduced-fat whole grain cookie	Beef and Vegetable Stew
7	Veggie and Cheese Omelette	Quinoa Salad with Chickpeas and Vegetables	One banana	Sweet Potato and Black Bean Soup

Week 20

Day	Breakfast	Lunch	Snack	Dinner
1	Veggie and Cheese Omelette	Spinach and Tofu Stir-Fry	One banana	Roasted Brussels Sprouts and Sweet Potatoes
2	Sweet Potato Breakfast Bowl	Baked Sweet Potato Fries with Avocado Dip	One apple	Chickpea and Spinach Curry
3	Whole Grain Porridge	Tuna Avocado Lettuce Wraps	Two sticks of celery filled with low-fat sof	Chickpea and Vegetable Stew
4	Overnight Oats with Chia Seeds and Berries	Lentil Soup with Vegetables	Reduced-fat whole grain cookie	Tuna Avocado Lettuce Wraps
5	Avocado Toast with Turkey Bacon	Chickpea and Veggie Salad	One rye cracker spread with low-fat soft chees	Spicy Shrimp and Avocado Salad
6	Sweet Potato Breakfast Bowl	Crab-Stuffed Avocado	One apple	Zucchini and Red Pepper Frittata
7	Vegetable Frittata	Roasted Brussels Sprouts and Sweet Potatoes	Reduced-fat whole grain cookie	Beef and Vegetable Stew

Week 21

Day	Breakfast	Lunch	Snack	Dinner
1	Avocado Toast with Turkey Bacon	Black Bean and Vegetable Soup	One pear	Roasted Pork Loin with Apple and Onion
2	Avocado Toast with Turkey Bacon	Turkey and Vegetable Stir-Fry	One pear	Mango and Black Bean Salad
3	Vegetable Frittata	Quinoa and Veggie Salad	One pear	Butternut Squash and Apple Soup
4	Overnight Oats with Chia Seeds and Berries	Pork Chops with Apple Chutney	One and a half ounces of dried apricots	Quinoa Salad with Chickpeas and Vegetables
5	Veggie Omelet	Grilled Tuna Salad	One orange	Chickpea and Spinach Curry
6	Sweet Potato Breakfast Bowl	Grilled Tuna Salad	One rye cracker spread with low-fat soft chees	Grilled Salmon with Roasted Asparagus
7	Veggie and Cheese Omelette	Chickpea and Sweet Potato Curry	One small banana	Pork Chops with Apple Chutney

CONCLUSION

Thank you for reaching the conclusion of this book. I hope you have learned a great deal about diabetes nutrition and diet. Now it is your responsibility to take care of your health. Remember that diabetes is not a life sentence, and it can be effectively managed so that you can enjoy all aspects of your life.

You must take care of yourself by consuming only natural foods and engaging in at least 30 minutes of daily physical activity.

Spread the word to your friends and family, and let's work together to raise awareness of diabetes, which we must manage and treat.

The best gift you can give yourself is good health! Wishing you the best!

MEASUREMENT CONVERSION CHART

Here are some conversion tables to help you measure recipes accurately.

CUPS	TBSP	TSP	ML
1	16	48	250
3/4	12	36	175
2/3	11	32	150
1/2	8	24	125
1/3	5	16	70
1/4	4	12	60
1/8	2	6	30
1/16	1	3	15

COOKING CONVERSION CHART

Measurement

CUP	ONCES	MILLILITERS	TABLESPOONS
8 cup	64 oz	1895 ml	128
6 cup	48 oz	1420 ml	96
5 cup	40 oz	1180 ml	80
4 cup	32 oz	960 ml	64
2 cup	16 oz	480 ml	32
1 cup	8 oz	240 ml	16
3/4 cup	6 oz	177 ml	12
2/3 cup	5 oz	158 ml	11
1/2 cup	4 oz	118 ml	8
3/8 cup	3 oz	90 ml	6
1/3 cup	2.5 oz	79 ml	5.5
1/4 cup	2 oz	59 ml	4
1/8 cup	1 oz	30 ml	3
1/16 cup	1/2 oz	15 ml	1

Temperature

FAHRENHEIT	CELSIUS
100 °F	37 °C
150 °F	65 °C
200 °F	93 °C
250 °F	121 °C
300 °F	150 °C
325 °F	160 °C
350 °F	180 °C
375 °F	190 °C
400 °F	200 °C
425 °F	220 °C
450 °F	230 °C
500 °F	260 °C
525 °F	274 °C
550 °F	288 °C

Weight

IMPERIAL	METRIC
1/2 oz	15 g
1 oz	29 g
2 oz	57 g
3 oz	85 g
4 oz	113 g
5 oz	141 g
6 oz	170 g
8 oz	227 g
10 oz	283 g
12 oz	340 g
13 oz	369 g
14 oz	397 g
15 oz	425 g
1 lb	453 g

Baking Measurements

If a recipe calls for this amount	You can also measure it this way
Dash	2 or 3 drops (liquid) or less than 1/8 teaspoon of (dry)
One tablespoon of	Three teaspoons or Half ounce
Two tablespoons of	1 ounce
A quarter cup of	Four tablespoons or 2 ounces
1/3 cup	Five tablespoons plus one teaspoon
Half cup of	Eight tablespoons or 4 ounces
3/4 cup	12 tablespoons of or 6 ounces
One cup of	16 tablespoons or 8 ounces
1 pint	2 cups or 16 ounces or 1 pound
1 quart	Four cups of or 2 pints
1 gallon	4 quarts
1 pound	16 ounces

Volume Measurements

US Units	Canadian Units	Australian Units
A quarter teaspoon of	1 ml	1 ml
Half teaspoon of	2 ml	2 ml
One teaspoon of	5 ml	5 ml
One tablespoon of	15 ml	20 ml
A quarter cup of	50 ml	60 ml
1/3 cup	75 ml	80 ml
Half cup of	125 ml	125 ml
2/3 cup	150 ml	170 ml
3/4 cup	175 ml	190 ml
One cup of	250 ml	250 ml
1 quart	1 liter	1 liter
One and a half quarts	One and a half liters	One and a half liters
2 quarts	2 liters	2 liters
Two and a half quarts	2.5 liters	2.5 liters
3 quarts	3 liters	3 liters
4 quarts	4 liters	4 liters

Weight Measurements

US Units	Canadian Metric	Australian Metric
1 ounce	30 grams	30 grams
2 ounces	55 grams	60 grams
3 ounces	85 grams	90 grams
4 ounces (1/4 pound)	115 grams	125 grams
8 ounces (half a pound)	225 grams	225 grams
16 ounces (1 pound)	455 grams	500 grams (half a kilogram)

Temperature Conversions

Fahrenheit	Celsius
32	0
212	100
250	120
275	140
300	150
325	160
350	180
375	190
400	200
425	220
450	230
475	240
500	260

Made in the USA
Las Vegas, NV
21 June 2023

73709962R00059